Legal Research:
How to Find and Understand the Law

Legal Research:
How to Find and Understand the Law

Suzanne McKie, LLB(Hons)
Barrister

Cavendish
Publishing
Limited

First published in Great Britain 1993 by Cavendish Publishing Limited,
23A Countess Road, London NW5 2XH.

Telephone: 071-485 0303   Facsimile: 071-485 0304

First published in the United States 1982 by Nolo Press.

British Library Cataloguing in Publication Data

McKie, Suzanne
Legal Research: How to Find and
  Understand the Law
I Title
344.20072

ISBN 1-874241-50-3

Printed and bound in Great Britain

Table of Contents

Chapter 1

How to Use this Book

Legal research comes in many forms and legal researchers have a myriad of faces. Recognising these two obvious facts, this book has been designed to be a flexible tool, of use to researchers of various levels of sophistication.

If you are new to legal research, start with Chapter 2 and work your way through the book. Chapter 2 will introduce you to an efficient and sensible method for approaching almost any legal research project. Chapter 3 provides an overview of our legal system. Chapters 4 to 11 show you how to:

- identify your research problem according to recognised legal categories;

- locate books that will give you an overview of the law that affects the particular issues with which you are concerned;

- find, read and understand the law itself: statutes, statutory instruments and cases;

- use the tools found in all law libraries—citators and digests— that enable you to find court opinions that address the issues you are interested in;

- organise the results of your research into a legal memorandum.

Appendices 1 and 2 provide real-life examples that put all the steps together and gives you a clear picture of how to solve a legal research problem. Chapter 12 provides a brief overview of computer-assisted legal research—what it is and how to use it.

If you already have some general legal research skills but want guidance on a particular aspect or phase, turn to the appropriate chapters and sections for a thorough explanation of a particular strategy.

Review questions following Chapters 2 to 10 help you focus on the important points you should know before going on. To the extent you need more in-depth information about a particular research tool or resource, your newly acquired skills will help you find it in the law library itself.

One last word. The best place to read this book is in a law library. Getting your hands on the books will make much of this book come alive in a way that the words, no matter how carefully chosen, cannot. You will benefit most by actually doing - one step at a time - the research examples set out in some of the chapters and by completing the research problems set out in the Appendices.

Chapter 2

An Overview of Legal Research

This chapter has two purposes: to give you some basic rules for efficient use of the law library and a basic legal research approach which will be useful for virtually any legal task. Once you understand how this overall approach works, any research task will be greatly simplified. Although some of what is said is fairly conventional (for example, keep accurate notes), much of it isn't.

A   Patience and Perspective

A certain type of attitude and approach are required to find the information you need efficiently among the billions of other legal facts and opinions in the law library. Probably the most important quality to cultivate is patience—a willingness to follow the basic legal research method diligently, even though it's a time-consuming process.

Unfortunately, many legal researchers are impatient, preferring to make a quick stab at finding the particular piece of information they think they need. While a quest for immediate gratification is sometimes appropriate when attempted by a master researcher, it most often results in no satisfaction at all when attempted by the less experienced.

Perhaps it will be easier to understand how legal research is best approached if we take an analogy from another field.

Seeking and finding information in a law library is a lot like learning how to cook a gourmet dish. To cook the dish you first need to settle on a broad category of cuisine—Japanese, French, Italian, etc. Next, you would find one or two good cookbooks that provide an overview of the techniques common to that specific cuisine. From there you would become more specific. You would find a recipe to your liking, learn the meaning of unfamiliar cooking terms and make a list of the ingredients. Finally, you would assemble the ingredients and carefully follow the instructions in the recipe.

Legal research also involves identifying a broad category before you search for more specific information. Once you know the general direction in which you are headed, you are prepared to find an appropriate background resource—an encyclopaedia, law journal, textbook—to educate yourself about the general issues involved in your research. Armed with this overview, you can then delve into the law itself—cases, statutes, statutory instruments—to find definitive answers to your questions. And, when your research is finished, you can pull your work together into a coherent written statement. (It is explained in Section D below that writing up your research is crucial to knowing whether you have finished.)

Of course, in the legal research process there are lots of opportunities for dead ends, misunderstandings and even mental deadlock. Answers that seemed in your hand five minutes ago evaporate when you read a later case or statutory amendment. Issues that seemed crystal clear become muddy with continued reading. As well as this, authoritative experts in a field often contradict each other.

Take heart. Even experienced legal researchers spend time exploring dead ends before they get on the right track. The truth is, most legal issues are confused and confusing—that's what makes them legal issues. Just remember that the main difference between the expert and novice researcher is that the expert has faith that sooner or later the research will result in something useful, while the novice too easily becomes convinced that the whole thing is hopeless. Fortunately, this book and many law librarians are there to help the struggling legal researcher.

B   A Basic Approach to Legal Research

The diagram on page 8 depicts the usual flow of legal research when you start from scratch. It is important to consider it before you get started. The details will be covered in later chapters, but it is clear from looking at it quickly that the legal researcher begins with a wealth of possibilities, and then narrows his or her search until a few relevant cases and/or statutes are found. In turn that law will allow the researcher to locate much additional and more recent law. Your greatest hope in the beginning will be to find a least one relevant case which answers your legal question completely. However, this goal is seldom, if ever, reached in reality. But, of course, the more relevant cases you can find the better your chance of nailing down a firm answer.

The diagram is intended for those who are setting out with an open-ended legal question, not for those who merely wish to check if a particular case has been cited in another case. The diagram is not meant to represent the only approach to legal research. It all depends on how much legal knowledge you already have, the time you have available, and the level of certainty you are after.

Overleaf is the diagram and the following are the steps indicated in it.

Step 1: Formulate your legal questions

It is important to start by knowing what you are looking for. For example, if someone has been bitten by a dog, break your legal research down into specific questions, such as:

1   Who is legally responsible for the injury caused by the dog?

2   What facts do I have to prove to bring an action against that person and win damages from them.

3   Does it make any difference if the dog has bitten anyone before?

4   Is there a statute, regulation or by-law which deals with dog bites?

What is vitally important to understand is that the way in which you formulate your legal questions in the beginning may determine the entire course of your research. Therefore it is always a good idea to consider rethinking your initial questions as your research progresses. For example, you may start out thinking that this is a case involving dangerous dogs, only to discover that it really involves the duties of a landowner to prevent harm from dangerous conditions on the land.

BASIC LEGAL RESEARCH METHOD CHART

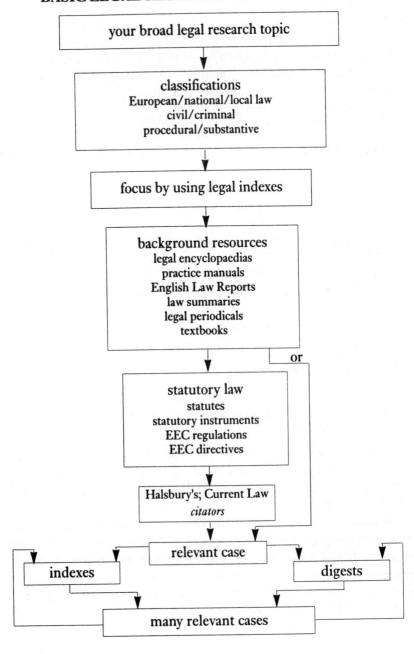

your broad legal research topic

classifications
European/national/local law
civil/criminal
procedural/substantive

focus by using legal indexes

background resources
legal encyclopaedias
practice manuals
English Law Reports
law summaries
legal periodicals
textbooks

or

statutory law
statutes
statutory instruments
EEC regulations
EEC directives

Halsbury's; Current Law
citators

relevant case

indexes

digests

many relevant cases

Step 2: Categorise your research questions

The next box down represents the classification stage. Because of the way legal materials are organised, it is usually necessary to place your research topic into a category described by using the three variables shown in this box. Exactly how this is accomplished is the primary subject of Chapter 4, *Putting your Questions into Legal Categories*.

Also covered in Chapter 4 is the next stage in the chart, when you break down your question into many words and phrases. That enables you to use legal indexes to find a background discussion of your topic.

Step 3: Find appropriate background resources

When starting a legal research task, you need an overview of the legal issues connected with your questions and an idea of how your questions fit into the larger legal fabric. This background information can normally best be obtained from books and articles, written by experts, that summarise and explain the subject. How to identify and use these background resources is covered in Chapter 5, *Obtaining Background Information*.

Step 4: Look for statutes

After you review background resources, you will want to proceed to the law itself. Usually, you should hunt for statutory law first. In most instances, the law starts with legislative or administrative enactments—statutes and rules—and ends with court decisions that interpret them. You too should usually deal with the statutory material first and the cases second. We show you how to research statutes in Chapter 6.

However, some important areas of the law are developed primarily in the courts—the law of personal injuries is a good example. If you have such a problem, and the background resource provides you with appropriate references, you might wish to start with cases first, and then come back and research statutory law if and when it is indicated. This alternative path is shown on the chart by the line that goes directly from 'Background Resources' to 'Relevant Case'.

Step 5: Look for cases

After finding one or more relevant statutes or rules, you will want to see how they have been interpreted by the courts. To pinpoint cases that discuss the statutory law you are interested in, use the tools listed in the next box: Halsbury's, Current Law, key words and phrases, and citators. These tools are addressed in Chapter 9, *Finding Cases*.

As soon as you find a case that fits in with your research question, you are almost home. This is because two major research tools cross-reference all cases by the issues decided in them. So if you find one case discussing your question, you can often quickly find several others discussing the same question.

Step 6: Check the case citators

Once you find a relevant case use a case citator, such as Current Law Case Citator or the Law Reports Index as these will enable you to discover if any other cases refer to it and so have a bearing on the question you require answering. These tools are covered in detail in Chapter 9.

Step 7: Update your legal research

Once you have found cases which are relevant to the question(s) which you have to answer, you will need to ensure that the cases still represent the law today. To do this you need to understand the issues involved in the cases, analyse each case for its value as precedent and use relevant digests and citators to locate more recent cases which bear on those issues. We show you how to do all of this in Chapters 7 to 9.

C   Five Time-Saving Research Tips

The research method just outlined, and the techniques explained in the rest of this book, work only if you proceed with method rather than madness. Otherwise, even though you know how to accomplish many legal research tasks, you are still likely to end up sifting through the law library book-by-book, spending many hours more than are necessary. In this context, here are five tips for more efficient legal research.

1   Check the layout of the law library

When first using a particular law library it is useful to give yourself a guided tour before you begin any legal research. Note the location of the major law reports, as well as Current Law, the Law Reports Index, Halsbury's Laws, Halsbury's Statutes, the Legal Journals Index, and the major practitioners' works. Sometime in the future you may need to discover the answer to something in a hurry. Most law libraries will have a map at reception or in the entrance room, but this cannot replace your own tour.

2   Take careful notes

Beginning any research exercise involves a certain amount of guesswork. You may make several false starts before finding the correct approach. Unfortunately it is human nature to be lazy on occasion and so you may find yourself repeating research already done. Therefore it is vitally important that you keep a track of all the steps you are taking, what cases you have considered and which digests, indexes, citators etc. you have looked through. It will save time in the long run.

3   Collect your materials in advance

As you check different cases and statutes for relevant material, you may find yourself reading only a few lines in many different books. So it is a good idea to make a list of all the books involved in the next phase of your research task and gather them in one place before you start reading. This allows you to find everything you need at once,which is far better than you continually jumping up and down. While this advice may seem obvious, apparently it isn't; you can observe the 'jump up and scurry' approach to legal research on any visit to the library.

4 Find a good law dictionary

Your legal research may introduce you to new terminology and knowing a good law dictionary will be very helpful. Here are two recommended dictionaries, which should be available in most law libraries:

Jowitt – *Dictionary of English Law* (Sweet & Maxwell) (2 volumes)

Stroud – *Stroud's Judicial Dictionary* (Sweet & Maxwell) (5 volumes)

5 Use the card or computer index

Each law library has a card and/or a computer index which list books, periodicals and statutory law available in the library. The indexes are usually organised by title or subject. The card index will be in alphabetical order and the cards themselves will usually state the location of the book, reports or journal in one corner of the card, and each library will display a 'map' explaining the cards.

The computer index is often quicker and more up-to-date. It is usually organised by subject, name, or word or phrase. Generally you will have to type in the relevant subject word, book title or author's name yourself. The screen will then display the relevant books, statutes or statutory instruments and their location, often with a brief summary of their contents. For example, if you wish to consider a possible action against a doctor for injuries caused to the potential plaintiff whilst undergoing surgery in hospital, enter 'SUBJECT' in the computer under 'library catalogue'. The computer will then allow you to type in the relevant subject title – here it would be 'PROFESSIONAL NEGLIGENCE' or

'MEDICAL NEGLIGENCE'. If your library holds nothing under these titles try a wider subject title, for example, 'NEGLIGENCE' or 'TORTS'. The computer will tell you how many items they hold under the title chosen, will list them, and tell you their location in that particular library.

Some law libraries even have a computerised daily law reports index, which allows you to type in a subject and obtain a list of cases under that title as reported in newspaper reports, generally, however, only from the last five or six years. This does make it a valuable tool for updating your research and will be considered in more detail later in Chapters 8, 9 and 12.

D   Always Know When You Have Finished

Legal research rarely produces an absolutely certain answer to a complicated question. Indeed, unless you are searching for a simple bit of information such as the maximum jail sentence for grievous bodily harm, trying to find the definitive answer to a legal research problem is often impossible.

There is a reason for this legal 'uncertainty principle.' Under the English legal system, any dispute that ends up in court is subject to the adversary process, where two or more parties fight it out and a judge or jury decides who should win. Of course, the fact that statutes are constantly produced and amended by the legislature and then subjected to judicial definition and redefinition substantially adds to the total confusion.

What all this means is that defining the 'law' that governs any set of facts almost by definition involves predicting how the courts would rule if presented with the question. If a prediction is based on clear statutes and court decisions, the level of uncertainty will be fairly low. However, if statutes and case law are themselves subject to conflicting interpretations, as many are, then even the best legal research may amount to little more than a sophisticated form of fortune-telling. Put another way, while in some instances you may believe you have found out 'what the law is,' a person with a different set of preconceptions will probably arrive at a different result.

Why mention legal uncertainty? Simply to warn you against trying to nail down an absolute answer to most legal questions. Often the best you can hope for is to understand the legal issues involved in a particular problem well enough to convince those who need to be convinced that your view is correct.

Once you understand your search for the truth will often stop short of absolute certainty, how can you tell when it is time to stop? To answer this question it is essential to develop a good sense of proportion and priorities.

Here are some questions to ask yourself in order to determine the answer to the big question, 'Have you finished?'

- *Have you logically answered the question you wanted answered when you began?* To test your answer, buttonhole a friend, post your question and then answer it on the basis of what your research disclosed. You will soon discover whether your logic holds up.

- *Are the laws and facts in the cases you have found pertinent to the facts of your situation?* To test your answer, decide whether the difference between the facts of your situation and the facts of any cases you have found (or those addressed by the statute you have located) could possibly make a difference in the answer to your question.

- *Are the materials you have found to support your answer as up-to-date as you can get?* Because law changes so rapidly, a case or statute that is only a year old may already be obsolete. You have not finished your research until you have checked all information to be sure it is current.

- *Have you used all major research resources that might improve your understanding or make your answer more certain?* If there are four different resources that might bear on a tax problem, it is wise to check all found rather than presuming any one to be correct.

- *Can you explain your reasoning in writing?* If your research is reasonably complete, you should be able to express in writing the question you researched, your answer to it and the basis for your answer. It is common to think you have finished a research task, only to discover when you try to write it up that there are gaping holes. Chapter 10 suggests some guidelines for putting your research results into written form, and the answers to the research problems in the appendices contain sample memoranda as examples.

If your answers to all the questions posed above is a resounding or even qualified 'yes,' then you have probably done about as much as possible. If you feel, however, that any of these questions deserves an honest 'no' or a waffling 'maybe,' you have more work to do.

REVIEW

Questions

1   What is your greatest hope when you begin a legal research task?

2   What are the seven basic steps to legal research?

3   How do you know when your legal research is finished?

Answers

1   To find at least one case and/or statute that perfectly — and favourably—answers your specific research question in an identical factual context.

2   Formulate your research questions.

`   Categorise your research questions.

    Find appropriate background resources.

    Look for statutes.

    Find a relevant case.

    Use citators and digests to find more cases.

    Use citators and indexes to update your research.

3   You have logically answered the question you wanted answered when you began.

    The laws and facts in the cases and statutes you have found are relevant to the particular facts of your situation.

    The materials you have found to support your answers are as up-to-date as you can find.

    You have utilised all the major research resources which might improve your understanding or make your answer more certain.

Chapter 3

An Overview of the Law

A   What is the Law?

We generally think of 'law' as the sum total of the rules governing individual and group behaviour that are enforceable in court. Primarily this means European law statutes, statutory instruments, local by-laws and court decisions. Added to this, however, are the decisions made by public bodies under a discretionary power, such as the refusal to award Housing Benefit to a particular individual, or the refusal of the police or the Crown Prosecution Service to prosecute a particular criminal.

Another view of the law is that it is subject to a higher, 'natural' law which applies to us as human beings. This is the law of what should happen—in a moral or ethical sense.

B   Foundations of English Law

Until the 12th century, law in the western world operated on several primary levels. Collections of written laws, such as the *Augustinian Code* or the *Code of Charlemagne* (both traceable to Roman law) created a broad written legal framework. This basic system still prevails in many countries and is known as the 'civil' law. In addition, the Catholic Church governed many activities under a large body of ecclesiastical law.

A legal tradition called the 'common' law quite different from that of the civil law, developed in England after the Norman conquest in 1066. At least since the reign of the great legal reformer Henry II in the 1100s, decisions by English grand juries, kings, magistrates and (slightly later) trial juries were written down and eventually catalogued according to the type of case. When the courts were called on to decide similar issues in subsequent cases, they reviewed the earlier decisions and, if one was found that logically covered the contemporary case, they applied the principle of the earlier decision. This doctrine is called *stare decisis*—Latin for 'let the decision stand.' The common law thus consists of court opinions in specific disputes that state legal principles and must usually be followed in subsequent court cases about the same type of dispute.

This does not mean that every judge's decision stands forever. Courts, however imperfectly, reflect society's values, and old case law may be rejected as society changes. The principle of *stare decisis* is, however, a strong one; judges are reluctant to discard well-established rules and take pains to explain (or deny) a significant departure from precedent.

Large areas of law are developed in England in this case-by-case common law tradition. Eventually, two basic types of courts evolved: the law courts and special 'chancery' courts established by the king to handle types of cases and provide types of relief that tradition did not allow the regular courts to entertain. The principles developed in the law courts were called 'legal' or 'law,' while the principles developed in the king's chancery courts were called 'equitable' or 'equity'. This distinction still exists in modern English law.

England also, beginning hesitantly with the Magna Carta in 1215, developed a parliamentary system under which statutes proposed by the king or his ministers were enacted by Parliament. These statutes were gathered together in books not too different from civil law codes.

C   The Increasing Importance of Statutes and Statutory Instruments

Over the centuries, the Common Law has been modified by statutes and statutory instruments, made thereunder. Both have become very important in making new law and codifying broad principles developed by the case law. When you are aware that a research problem involves statutory law, this is your first port of call. The researcher should never consider the case law before reading the words of the statute extremely carefully, or before reading any statutory instruments relevant to the particular issue under consideration. If you have no idea if the answer involves statutory law, your first stop will be a background resource, such as a practitioner's manual, a textbook or legal encyclopaedia. These will tell you if the issue does involve such law.

D   The Increasing Importance of European Law

Article 2 of the Treaty of Rome states that the European Community has as its task the establishing of a common market and progressive approximation of the economic policies of the Member States (of which England is one); the promotion throughout the Community of a harmonious development of economic activities, a continuous and balanced expansion, an increase in stability, an accelerated raising of the standard of living and closer relations between the States belonging to it.

Article 3 details the activities of the Community, including the adoption of a common policy in the sphere of agriculture and transport; and the approximation of the laws of the Member States to the extent required for the proper functioning of the common market.

As for actual law, the EEC, or rather the European Council and the European Commission, produces directives and regulations. Case law is produced by the judgments of the European Court of Justice. The EEC Treaty has created its own legal system which is an integral part of the of the legal systems of the member states. Directly applicable Community Law, however, prevails over inconsistent domestic law of those member states. A 'regulation' produced by the EEC is directly applicable in its entirety, and does not require a process of implementation or adoption in the different member states. A 'directive', on the other hand, does require implementation. The judgments of the European Court of Justice are binding on the member states but do not always give individuals new rights against their own states.

The areas of English law which may involve European law include:

Commercial law

Constitutional law

Consumer protection law

Employment law

Food and drugs law

Law of International trade

Public law

Sex discrimination law.

For some areas of law, it is worth considering also the European Convention on Human Rights. This has not been implemented into English law as yet, but the English courts will, on the whole, take it into account. It contains, *inter alia*, the following rights and freedoms:

The right to life (Article 2)

The freedom from torture or inhuman or degrading treatment or punishment (Article 3)

The freedom from slavery and forced labour (article 4)

The right to a fair trial (Article 6)

The individual's right to privacy (Article 8)

The right to freedom of thought and religion (Article 9)

The right to freedom of expression (Article 10)

The right to freedom of assembly and association (Article 11)

E   The Development of English Common Law

Despite the increasing importance of statutory law, many areas of our law still consist almost entirely of court decisions. Also, the courts of this country are allowed to interpret statutory law when a dispute arises as to its meaning. As well as using other interpretive techniques, a judge will look at earlier cases to see how the law has been interpreted in the past and apply the prevailing interpretation unless he or she feels it is plainly wrong. In other words, court opinions serve as authorities or precedents, which are generally binding. All courts in the English legal system must follow decisions of the court above. All but the House of Lords must follow their own previous decisions unless plainly wrong.

The courts whose decisions are published are usually the High Court, the Court of Appeal and the House of Lords. The decisions of Crown Courts, Magistrates Courts and the County Court are less frequently published, as these courts are more likely to deal with questions of fact as opposed to law.

Interpretive techniques

When a court needs to interpret statutory law, they should look at the statute or statutory instrument itself which may include a definition section or paragraph.

Other interpretation techniques include the somewhat basic task of referring to a dictionary for the ordinary meanings of words where there is no legal definition available either in the statute or elsewhere. The Interpretation Act 1978 contains definitions for standard legal terms, for example 'man' includes 'woman', and the singular includes the plural, unless the statutory provision declares otherwise.

Another useful resource for interpretation is the textbook by Bennion, 'Statutory Interpretation', published by Butterworths. This is a very thorough and detailed source of information.

Finally, as a result of the recent case of *Pepper v Hart* [1992] 3 WLR 1032, the House of Lords has decided that where the legislation is ambiguous, courts can now refer to Hansard, in order to determine the purpose of the legislation concerned. Hansard reports the speeches made to parliament of the promoter of the legislation, and any relevant debate. According to *Pepper*, if the promoter clearly states the meaning behind the statute or a section of it, this can be considered by the court. Hansard is available in most law libraries.

F   From Where English Law is Derived

Laws are made at three basic levels:- European, national and local. Operating at these levels are three sources of law:- the legislature, judges and executive officers, the latter usually acting through government bodies. See the chart set out below. The following chapter provides some tips on how to decide which source of law controls your issue.

Sources of law
- European Regulations
- European Directives
- Decisions of the European Court of Justice
- National Statutory law, passed by Parliament
- Statutory Instruments, or regulations, made under statutes
- English case law, as decided by English courts of law
- Local by-laws, created by local government bodies

G   Going to Court

The actual procedure involved in civil and criminal trials is outside the realms of this book. However, it is important to know when and how to present statutory law and case law when in court.

i) Tribunals

When at a tribunal the bench will usually prefer it if you do not refer to a great deal of case law, as they see themselves as concerned with the finding of facts rather than determinants of the law. However, if you feel the need to state the law then you should be ready to have photocopies at the ready for each member of the bench (usually three) as well as a copy for your opponent. You can usually hand these up as you refer to them. Photocopies of the relevant parts of a statute or statutory instruments can also be used in the same way, but it should be accepted that in general the bench will know the basic law.

As for Appeal Tribunals, these are concerned with the law, as they consider appeals from the first stage industrial tribunals. Photocopies can be used in the same way, or you can send a list of your cases, with citations, to the court at least a day before the hearing.

ii) At trial and at other hearings

Again, as most trials are concerned with fact-finding you will not often refer to statutory or case law. However, occasionally it will be necessary. For example during a *voir dire* (a trial within a trial) in a criminal case, you may wish to refer to case law in order to suggest how a judge should exercise his discretion when deciding whether or not to exclude a confession made by the defendant.

In the Magistrates courts, it is generally sufficient to pass up photocopies to the magistrates, as well as a copy for your opponent. By contrast, in the Crown Court, the court should be told of which case and statutory law you intend to refer to, at least the afternoon of the day before the case or submission begins. As a matter of courtesy, your opponent should also be given a list of your authorities the day before.

In civil cases, if the value of your contractual or tortious claim is less than one thousand pounds it will go to small claims arbitration, an informal way of resolving disputes, and so it is unlikely that any sort of law will be referred to. Below £50,000, a contractual or tortious case is most likely to be tried in the County Court; above that, in the High Court. Particularly in the High Court, a list of authorities should be given to the court, and to your opponent, the day before. The court may have the relevant law reports and digests and, therefore, their own copies, but not always. Your opponent may bring along his own copies, but this may not always be the case. Copies should be made available by you for the court and for your opponent. If you are served with a list of authorities yourself you should consider the cases and statutory law before the hearing.

iii) On appeal

When appealing against a decision in the House of Lords or Court of Criminal or Court of Civil Appeal, the above applies in the same way Many advocates produce skeleton arguments which will be sent to the court and to their opponent(s) the day before. These will usually include any authorities upon which the advocate intends to rely.

REVIEW

Questions

1   What does the Common Law consist of?

2   What does *stare decisis* mean?

3   How is power shared between Europe, England and local government?

Answers

1   The Common Law consists of court opinions in specific disputes that state legal principles and must usually be followed in subsequent court cases involving the same type of dispute.

2   *Stare decisis* is Latin for 'let the decision stand.' When the courts were called on to decide similar issues in subsequent cases, they reviewed the earlier decisions and, if one was found which logically covered the contemporaneous case, they applied the principle of the earlier decision. This is how the Common Law developed.

3   European Community Regulations prevail over inconsistent national law and covers such areas of law as employment law, food and drugs, consumer protection and discrimination law. European law is also derived from directives from the Commission and case law of the European Court of Justice.

    The English, or national law, is supreme in all areas of law not touched by the law of the European Community. In many areas of law the European Community has no part to play; for example, criminal law and trusts law. English law is derived from statutes, statutory instruments and case law.

Local by-laws are not statutory instruments, but rules created by local authorities governing such things as law relating to litter, noise pollution and planning.

Chapter 4

Putting your Questions into Legal Categories

This chapter helps you accomplish Step 2 of the legal research method (described in Chapter 2). First, it shows how to organise your legal question into the conceptual categories used by law book publishers, a necessary and preliminary step to finding appropriate background resources (which are covered in the next chapter). Second, this chapter introduces you to some techniques for using legal indexes. Legal indexes are most commonly used to find:

- relevant discussions in the background resources you select

- statutes in annotated series (Chapter 6), and

- cases through the case digest system (Chapters 8 and 9).

A Find the Broad Legal Category for your Problem

Assume that you seek a lawyer's advice because you injured your back when you slipped on a banana skin at the supermarket. An experienced lawyer will go through a thought process which, if verbalised, might sound something like this:

'Ah, let's see, this person slipped, fell and injured herself, possibly badly. Back injuries cause a lot of pain—that means high damages. Definitely it is a personal injury case, a civil matter, negligence. Let's see, in order to recover for negligence, some action or inaction on the part of the supermarket must have been wrongful. In this situation it probably wasn't an intentional tort, but more likely carelessness, or negligence. Whether the market was negligent probably depends on how long employees let the banana skin remain on the floor before the accident. I wonder if there were any prior occurrences like this?'

This exercise demonstrates how lawyers love to reduce problems to smaller parts and to classify the parts according to familiar—to them—legal jargon. While this process may seem a little intimidating if you are unfamiliar with the law, do not worry. Anybody can learn to break a legal research problem into its appropriate topics and sub-topics. As mentioned earlier, once you are able to place the proper labels on various factual situations, your ability to perform meaningful legal research will be almost assured. You may be surprised at how easy classification really is.

There are four main questions to answer when classifying your legal question:

- Does it involve European law, national law, or local law?
- Does it involve criminal law or civil law?
- Does it involve the substance of the law or legal procedure?
- What legal category does it belong in?

When you have answered each of these questions you will find it much easier to choose the right background resources to look at. If your question involves the substance of the criminal law, you will be interested in one group of books; if it involves national civil law, you will be looking for others. Narrowing your search further, placing your question in the right category will tell you which specific books—and parts of the books—you need. For instance, if your law problem involves the national drug laws, you will probably use a different book or different section than if it involves mortgage fraud.

1 Does the situation involve European, national or local law?

This is one of the most important primary questions you must ask yourself when first embarking on legal research. The chart below lists the topics usually covered by European, national and local law.

a) European law

Commercial law

Constitutional law

Consumer protection law

Employment law

Law of International Trade

Public law

Sex discrimination law

Law of Euro-torts

All of the above are also governed in part by national law.

b) National law

All of the above and all other areas of law, such as criminal law, family law, trusts, land law, company law, contract law, landlord and tenant, police law, probate, torts, tax and insolvency.

c) Local law

Litter

Noise pollution

Planning

Waste Pollution

Local government bodies have the power to enact certain local bye-laws, covering areas of law not covered by European or national law at all or with sufficient particularity. For example, bye-laws prohibiting littering the pavement, and allowing the local body to demand a fine; bye-laws prohibiting smoking on the underground, with a fine attached; and planning laws not governed by national law.

2　Does the situation involve criminal law or civil law?

This is a very important distinction to make as it is necessary to determine which your situation involves before turning to the background resources.

a) Criminal law

Generally, if a certain type of behaviour is punishable by imprisonment or the imposition of a fine, paid into public funds, then criminal law is involved. Criminal charges are usually initiated by the police, and then the Crown Prosecution Service, or local authorities, such as with Trading Standards cases. Private prosecutions are also possible. The easiest way to determine if the situation involves criminal law is to check *Archbold on Pleading, Practice and Evidence* (Sweet and Maxwell), Volume Two.

b) Civil law

All legal questions that do not involve criminal law involve the civil law. When an action is started in the courts over a broken contract, custody of a child or a negligent physical injury, civil law is involved. In a civil action, the court may be asked to issue orders, award damages or dissolve a marriage. Imprisonment is only very rarely ordered.

3 Is the problem substantive or procedural?

Primarily for legal analysis and classification, the law has been divided into two large sub-groups. One of these includes all law which establishes the rights we enjoy and the duties we owe to the government, to other people and to entities and the duties the government gives to us. This type of law is often referred to as 'substantive' law. The other major sub-group includes all law that governs the way the system of justice works. This law is known as 'procedural' law.

Once you determine which sub-group covers your situation the easier it will be to begin your legal research. For example, the police search a person's home without a warrant, and without reference to the law of the Police and Criminal Evidence 1984, and discover drugs as a result. Your research may involve looking at the substantive law in relation to the offence of possession of drugs, but will also involve researching the procedural law in relation to the exclusion or non-exclusion of evidence as a result of such a search under the common law and under the above-mentioned statute.

a) Criminal Law

The major criminal law substantive categories:

Offences against property, eg theft, fraud

Public order offences

Road traffic offences

Offences under the Offences Against the Person Act

Drugs offences

Kidnapping

Homicide

Tax evasion

Firearms offences

Trade description, consumer protection and food offences

Contempt offences

Obscene publications

Perjury

Official secrets

Child abduction

Terrorist offences

Sexual offences

The major criminal procedural categories:

Arrests

Bail

Charging

Police detention and questioning

Laying information

Indictments

Extradition

Committal for trial

The trial process

The jury verdict

Summing up by the judge

Pleas

Pre-sentence reports

Sentencing

Search and seizure

Suppression of evidence

Trial of juveniles

Appeals

Ancillary financial and property orders

Licensing

4 Substantive civil law categories

The list set out below contains some of the more common substantive civil law categories utilised by the law books. While some of these areas overlap and may be used interchangeably by book titles and indexes, if you can assign one or more of the categories to your problem, it will be much easier for you to find what you are looking for. If you cannot get your problem to fit within one of these categories, do not despair. If you cannot find a background resource which covers your area of law, use the digests and indexes discussed in Chapters 8 and 9 to start your research.

Administrative Law The law governing how administrative agencies function. This includes: the procedures used by agencies when they issue regulations, the way agencies conduct hearings, the scope of authority granted agencies by the legislature, and how agencies enforce their policies, decisions and regulations. The law also explains how an individual can challenge the decisions of public bodies.

Bankruptcy Who can use the bankruptcy courts and under what circumstances; the rules and procedures used by the bankruptcy courts when a person or business files a bankruptcy petition to cancel debts or restructure them so as to continue operations; which debts are subject to cancellation or restructuring and how any remaining assets of the person declaring bankruptcy are distributed.

Commercial Law The law governing commercial relations between borrowers and lenders, banks and their customers, wholesalers and retailers, mortgagors and mortgagees etc. Generally, this area involves disputes between business-people rather than between a business-person and a consumer. (See Consumer Law.)

Computer Law The various issues that are especially relevant to the manufacture, use and sale of computers and computer software. This area includes such topics as copyrighting and patenting of computer software, warranties connected with computer sales, use of computer-generated documents in court, access to computerised files, privacy in connection with computer databases, computer-related crimes and trade secret protection in the computer industry.

Constitutional Law All situations where the constitutionality of governmental action is called into question.

Consumer Law Law governing transactions between a seller and a buyer of personal property in a commercial setting. This field typically involves situations where persons buy items on hire-purchase—such as cars, household furniture or electronic equipment—and a dispute arises as to whether the buyer was provided with sufficient notice of what the transaction actually involved or—if the goods did not work—whether the seller is responsible under a warranty or guarantee.

Contracts Written and oral agreements, when such agreements are enforceable, when they may be broken, and what happens if they are broken. Contract law is primarily concerned with general questions of contract law rather than with specific types of contracts. For specific types of contracts, see Consumer Law, Commercial Law, Landlord and Tenant Law, Intellectual Property Law and Employment Law.

Company Law How corporations are formed, the requirements for corporate structure, the rights of shareholders, the rights and duties of corporate officers and directors, the relationship between a corporation and outside parties who commercially interact with it, procedures for elections of officers, how stock is issued, and similar matters.

Discrimination Law Statutes and European provisions that apply to discrimination on the basis of such characteristics as race, sex, ethnic or national background, or colour. (See also Landlord and Tenant Law and Prison Law.)

Employment Law The rights of employees and the restrictions placed on employers by law. This area is also concerned with employment discrimination against minorities (see also Discrimination Law), wrongful dismissal of employees and management labour relations.

Environmental Law The numerous statutes, EEC and national regulations and cases that govern the uses of the environment by businesses, government and individuals. Issues of air and water pollution, the environmental impact of new projects, the uses of national forests and parks, the preservation of endangered species, toxic and nuclear wastes and similar matters are covered under this topic.

Equity / Probate and Trusts Law How people arrange for the distribution of their property after they are dead, and how they can avoid paying taxes and probate fees by taking certain actions while they are living. Includes such subjects as living trusts, joint tenancies, wills, testamentary trusts and gifts.

Evidence What kinds of items and testimony can be introduced as proof in a trial or hearing, the methods used to introduce such proof and how much weight the trier of fact (judge or jury) should give different types of proof.

Family law, Divorce Law, Domestic Relations Law All matters relating to annulment, marriage, separation, divorce, taxation upon divorce, child support, child custody, child contact, marital property, community property, guardianships, adoptions and local authority care.

Health Law The type and quality of medical treatment received from hospitals, health facility regulation and planning, occupational health and safety requirements, rural and neighbourhood health clinics, the control of pesticide use and other issues related to health.

Intellectual Property Law The laws and procedures governing copyrights, trademarks, trade secrets and patents.

Landlord and Tenant Law Concerned with all issues arising out of the landlord-tenant relationship, such as evictions, responsibility for repairs, deposits, leases and rental agreements, inspections, entries by the landlord, liability for injuries, rent control and similar matters.

Media Law The laws and requirements that pertain to the print and broadcast media, and includes such items as libel, privacy, censorship, access to government information and court records, licensing of radio and television stations and restrictions on television and radio programming.

Prison Law Prison conditions, prison disciplinary procedures, parole, constitutional rights of prisoners and adequate access to legal information and medical treatment. (These issues are also often found under the Civil Procedure, Criminal Procedure and Constitutional Law categories.)

Property Law The purchase, maintenance and sale of real estate, easements, adverse possession, landowner's liability, mortgages and deeds of trust, and issues arising from land use regulation.

Public Utilities Law The duties, responsibilities and rights of public utilities that provide water, telephone service, sewage and refuse disposal, and gas and electricity.

Tax Law All issues related to such items as income, property left in an estate, personal property, business profits, real estate, and sales transactions.

Tort Law Any injury to a person or property that is directly caused by the intentional or negligent actions of another. Examples of commonly known intentional torts, where the person intends the act and knew or should have known that it would result in someone being injured, are:

- assault (including putting another in reasonable fear of being struck);

- battery (the objectionable touching of another without his or her consent);

- libel and slander (a false statement made to someone about a third person that has the capacity to hurt the third person's reputation or business);

- trespass (entering onto another's property without consent or legal justification);

- false imprisonment (restricting a person's freedom of movement without legal justification);

- malicious prosecution (prosecuting a person without just cause for ulterior motives).

The most common tort of all is called 'negligence'. This involves behaviour that is considered unreasonably careless under the circumstances and which directly results in injury to another or his property. In deciding whether a given activity is unreasonably careless, the courts must determine whether it was reasonably foreseeable that the kind of injury suffered by the plaintiff would result from the act alleged to be negligent.

B   Identify Specific Terms for your Problem

Most law books contain indexes organised by subject. These indexes are usually quite specific, and you almost always have to use them in your legal research. You have got off to a good start by putting your problem into a broad legal category. But you must now become more specific.

There are no hard and fast rules for how indexes are set up and what headings are used. How well an individual index is organised depends so much upon the knowledge and effort of the person making it that indexing is recognised as an art form. One index might refer to divorces under the 'domestic relations' category, while another might use the term 'family law' to designate the broad category. Still a third index might use only the word 'divorce'.

Most people—especially those unfamiliar with the law—experience difficulty when first faced with a legal index. This, of course, is because the indexes themselves often use legal jargon. For instance, the law on the subject of whether more than one person can be sued in one lawsuit is typically indexed under 'Joinder of Parties'. Some would not think of looking there unless they were already familiar with the term.

Also, indexes can be quite unpredictable when it comes to more specific matters. For example, suppose you wanted to find out who is responsible for the back injury that resulted from your slip and fall at the supermarket. After some cross-referencing by using the list of civil topics in Section A4 of this chapter, you might realise that you were dealing with a 'tort'. Where would you go next, however?

Under this general category, would you look under 'slip', 'fall', 'back injury', 'liability', 'duty of care', 'negligence' or 'supermarket'? Most likely 'duty of care' or 'negligence'.

The trick in using an index well mostly involves being able to come up with many alternative words that describe or relate to your research topic. Put simply, the more words you can think of, the better your chances of finding what you are looking for.

Many legal indexes use ordinary as well as legal words for their headings, and contain elaborate cross-indexing systems so that even if you do not choose the right word to begin with, you will finally get to it through cross-reference entries. Good indexes cross-reference every significant term so that if the primary information is carried under 'family law', for example, the word 'divorce' would have 'see family law' under it.

Several legal research experts have constructed methods for breaking a legal research problem down into words and phrases that can be looked up in a legal index. Probably the most complete method is that employed by American professor of law William Statsky.

1   The Statsky 'cartwheel' approach

The Statsky approach uses a diagram—called a cartwheel—which prompts the reader for different categories of words.

For example, suppose that the research problem involved, among other things, considering who is authorised to perform a wedding and what ceremony, if any, need be conducted. The structure of the Cartwheel is shown on page 43.

The Research Cartwheel

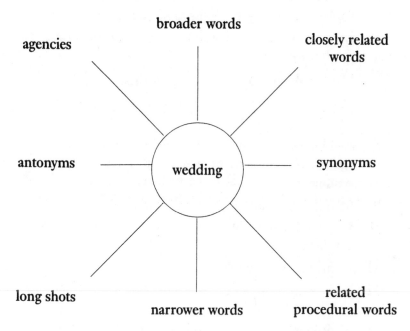

Reproduced by permission from Domestic Relations by William P. Statsky, copyright © 1978 by West Publishing Company. All Rights Reserved

The first step in using the index and table of contents in any law book is to look up the key word—'wedding' in this case—in that index and table. If that is not successful, either because the word is not in the index or table, or because the page or section references after the word in the index and table do not lead to relevant material in the book, the next step is to think of as many different words related to 'wedding' as possible.

The Cartwheel method has 18 steps to help you think of related terms to look up in an index or table of contents. It is, in effect, a word association game which should become second nature to you with practice.

1   Identify all the major words from the facts of the research problem. Place each word or small set of words in the centre of the Cartwheel.

2   In the index and table of contents, look up all of these words.

3   Identify the broader categories of these major words.

4   In the index and table of contents, look up all of these broader categories.

5   Identify the narrower categories of these words.

6   In the index and table of contents, look up all of the narrower categories.

7   Identify all of the synonyms of the words.

8   In the index and table of contents, look up all of these synonyms.

9   Identify all of the antonyms of these words.

10 In the index and table of contents, look up all of these antonyms.

11 Identify all closely related words.

12 In the index and table of contents, look up all of these closely related words.

13 Identify all procedural terms related to these words.

14 In the index and table of contents, look up all of these procedural terms.

15 Identify all agencies, if any, which might have some connection to these words.

16 In the index and table of contents, look up all of these agencies.

17 Identify all long shots.

18 In the index and table of contents, look up all of these long shots.

If we were to apply these 18 steps of the Cartwheel to the word 'wedding', here are some of the words and phrases that you would check in the index and table of contents of every law book that deals with family law.

Agencies church, registry office, ministry, vicar, priest.

Broader Words celebration, ceremony, rite, ritual, formality, festivity

Narrower Words civil wedding, church wedding, shotgun marriage

Synonyms marriage, nuptial

Antonyms alienation, annulment, dissolution, divorce, separation

Loosely Related Words matrimony, marital, domestic, husband, wife, bride, anniversary, custom, children, blood test, premarital, spouse, relationship, family, home, consummation, cohabitation, sexual relations, minister, wedlock, oath, contract, name change, domicile, residence.

Procedural Terms application, petition, ancillary proceedings, licence.

Long Shots dowry, common law, single, blood relationship, fraud, religion, illegitimate, remarriage, prenuptial, maintenance, bigamy, pregnancy, gifts, chastity, property, impotence, incest, virginity, support, custody, consent, paternity.

Perhaps you might think that some of the word selections in the above categories are a bit farfetched. But you simply will not know for sure whether or not a word will be fruitful until you try it. To be successful, you must be imaginative. By simply finding one related term or phrase, you will open up a cornucopia of additional leads. A thesaurus can also be helpful in stimulating your imagination.

Understanding words used in an index

Indexes use jargon that may be quite confusing if you're new to them. Here are some definitions of some of the more commonly used terms.

'see also'

The terms following the 'see also' may produce related subject matter.

'see'

The material you are seeking will be found directly under the term following the 'see' rather than under the original term.

'see *infra*'

The entry is found under the same main entry but further down alphabetically. It's Latin for 'below'.

'see *supra*'

The entry is found under the same main entry, but further up alphabetically. It's Latin for 'above'.

2 An informal approach

If you do not want to follow the Cartwheel method, there are other ways to approach legal indexes. The one that we use most of the time has six steps:

Step 1 Select several key plain-English terms that define the research problem, and several alternatives to these terms.

Step 2 Use these words to select one or more probable legal categories

Step 3 Search the index for a main entry relevant to your problem and be prepared to follow up cross-references.

Step 4 Search for relevant sub-entries under the main entry.

Step 5 Bounce back to another main entry if your first choice is not productive.

Step 6 Once you find a good main entry and sub-entry, think in an even smaller and more detailed manner.

For instance, suppose your research question is whether a drink driving conviction results in the loss of a driver's licence. The first step is to determine some key terms. You might start with 'drink driving' and such variations as 'operating a motor vehicle under the

[456]

General Index from 'Archbold'

INDEX

General Index from 'Archbold'

influence of intoxicating beverages' or 'driving while intoxicated'. The same process would hold true for 'driver's licence'. Possible alternative terms for driver's licence are 'operator's permit' or 'operator's licence'. These terms may be too specific to be dealt with as main headings in an index and so you would go onto the second step.

The second step is to determine whether these terms logically fit under one of the general civil or criminal law substantive categories. Road traffic law would be the most appropriate category, so you would probably start with 'vehicles' under 'Road Traffic Law'.

The third step is to search the index and be prepared to follow up cross-references. For instance, in this example, if you started with 'vehicles', you would probably be referred to 'motor vehicles'.

The fourth step is to search for sub-entries under an appropriate main entry. For instance, if you looked for drink driving under motor vehicles, you might find an alternative term, such as 'operating under the influence'.

The fifth step is to go back to another main entry if your first choice is not productive. For example, if you found no reference to 'drink driving' or its equivalent under 'motor vehicles', consider looking under 'alcohol', 'traffic offences', 'alcoholic beverages' or 'automobiles'. You also might come up with some more variations of your specific terms.

The sixth step is to conceptualise even more detailed entries that are likely to refer you to material on your specific question. For instance, once you find an entry that covers drink driving under the main entry motor vehicles, you might consider looking for such specific terms as 'licence', suspension', 'revocation', 'restriction', 'forfeiture' and 'disqualification'.

If you run up against a brick wall, take a deep breath and start again. Reconsider your question, come up with new terms, find a different substantive category. The reason most research fails is that the researcher runs out of patience at the index searching stage.

REVIEW

Questions

1   Why is it necessary to fit your research problems into certain legal categories?

2   What are the four main questions to answer when categorising your legal question?

3   What are the main legal categories that usually involve a point of European law?

4   What are the legal categories that involve national law?

5   What are some legal categories that involve a point of local law?

6   What is the main way you can tell whether a research issue involves criminal law or civil law?

7   What is the difference between substantive law and procedural law?

8   What is the first step to using the informal index-searching method?

Answers

1   The books (background resources) you begin your research with are organised in this way.

2   Does it involve European law, national law or local law?

    Does it involve criminal law, civil law or both?

    Does it involve substantive law or procedural law?

    If it involves substantive law, what is the appropriate sub-topic?

    If it involves procedural law, what is the appropriate sub-topic?

3   Constitutional law, consumer protection law, food and drugs law, employment law, international trade, and sex discrimination law.

4   All of the above, plus criminal law, torts, family law, trusts, probate, contract law, company law, land law, landlord and tenant, tax law and insolvency law.

5   Planning; pollution; litter and safety regulations.

6   If the research issue involves behaviour that is generally punishable by imprisonment or a fine, then criminal law is involved. Civil law covers everything else, for example, cases of a broken contract, personal injury, divorce or other dispute where the court is asked to issue orders, award damages or dissolve a marriage.

7   Substantive law consists of numerous sets of principles that determine the rights and duties of an individual or body. Procedural law is concerned with how our legal system works—that is such matters as which courts are appropriate for certain types of dispute, what papers need to be filed with the court, who can be sued, and thediscovery and exchange of documents.

8   Select several key ordinary words that define the research problem, and several related alternatives to these terms.

Chapter 5

Obtaining Background Information

A   How Background Resources Can Help

Once you have tentatively classified your problem, and so placed it in a particular niche, you are now ready to find some answers to that problem. First you need to find the appropriate background resource or resources, and then you can use your legal index skills to find helpful discussions within the resources available. Use the computerised catalogue available in most law libraries - type in a subject area (as listed below) and you will see the titles of any relevant background resources produced on screen, along with their position in the library.

B   Background Resources for Law Students

Many books published as textbooks for students offer an excellent point of departure for legal research. These books, which are conceptual in nature, are excellent if you want a basic understanding of the variables in any specific area of concern. They are not always useful in providing a specific answer to a specific question, nor will they provide all the up-to-date information you may need. Below is a partial list of some commonly used and relatively up-to-date student textbooks.

SELECTED TEXTBOOKS

Administrative Law

Wade - 'Administrative Law' (Clarendon Press)

Agency

Markesinis and Munday - 'An Outline of the law of Agency' (Butterworths)

Civil Procedure

O'Hare and Hill - 'Civil Litigation' (Longman)

Commercial Law

Goode – 'Commercial Law' (Pelican)

Constitutional Law

de Smith –'Constitutional and Administrative law' (Pelican)

Company

Farrar – 'Farrar's Company Law' (Butterworths)

Pennington – 'Pennington's Company Law' (Butterworths)

Contract Law

Treitel – 'The Law of Contract' (Sweet & Maxwell)

Criminal Law

Smith and Hogan – 'Criminal Law' (Butterworths)

Criminal Procedure

Emmins – 'A Practical Approach to Criminal Procedure' (Blackstone Press Ltd.)

Employment Law

Smith and Wood – 'Industrial Law' (Butterworths)

Evidence

Keane – 'The Modern Law of Evidence' (Butterworths)

Family Law

Cretney and Masson – 'Principles of Family Law' (Sweet & Maxwell)

Intellectual Property

Cornish – 'Intellectual Property: Patents, Copyright, Trade Marks and Allied Rights' (Sweet & Maxwell)

Land Law

Gray – 'Elements of Land Law' (Butterworths)

Landlord and Tenant

Evans and Smith – 'The Law of Landlord and Tenant' (Butterworths)

Media Law

Robertson and Nicol – 'Media Law' (Penguin Books)

Sale of Goods and Consumer Protection

Macleod – 'Consumer Sales Law' (Butterworths)

Dobson –'Sale of Goods and Consumer Credit' (Sweet & Maxwell)

Torts

Salmond and Heuston – 'The Law of Torts' (Sweet & Maxwell)

Winfield and Jolowicz – ' Torts' (Sweet & Maxwell)

Trusts

Hanbury and Maudsley – 'Modern Equity' (Stevens & Sons)

C   Background Resources for Practitioners

There are lots of books designed to educate practising lawyers about the 'ins' and 'outs' of various legal subjects. They are usually very specific and provide plenty of case citations and, quite often, make reference to articles in law reviews and other periodicals. These background resources will refer you to the primary sources of law, that is cases, statutes or statutory instruments on which the discussion is based. Put simply, these background resources provide not only a conceptual overview of your research problem, but also an excellent bridge from your background reading to the next stage of your research - the primary sources of the law. The most common of these background resources are discussed in this section.

i) *Legal Encyclopaedias*

Legal Encyclopaedias are available for many areas of law, and contain detailed discussions of a particular area of law. They usually contain a thorough index, and appendices containing copies of statutes and statutory instruments. As well as this, loose-leaf pamphlets are produced several times a year which contain the latest law.

Legal Encyclopaedias are a good starting point for the legal researcher as they contain the statutory law, caselaw and commentary. Many have two or more volumes, but don't be put off by this - as long as you use the index properly you will discover how easy they are to use. Some examples of the most widely used Encyclopaedias are given below.

British Tax Encyclopaedia (Sweet & Maxwell)

Encyclopaedia of Banking Law (Butterworths)

Encyclopaedia of Consumer Credit Law (Sweet & Maxwell)

Encyclopaedia of Data Protection (Sweet & Maxwell)

Encyclopaedia of Environmental Health (Sweet & Maxwell)

Encyclopaedia of European Patent Law (Sweet & Maxwell)

Encyclopaedia of Financial Services Law (Butterworths)

Encyclopaedia of Health and Safety at Work (Sweet & Maxwell)

Encyclopaedia of Housing (Law and Practice) (Sweet & Maxwell)

Encyclopaedia of Local Government Law (Sweet & Maxwell)

Encyclopaedia of Planning (Law and Practice) (Sweet & Maxwell)

Encyclopaedia of Professional Partnerships (Sweet & Maxwell)

Encyclopaedia of Road Traffic (Sweet & Maxwell)

Encyclopaedia of VAT (Sweet & Maxwell)

ii) Law Reports

There are several law reports available for the practitioner to use. The majority have a useful subject index which categorise the cases to be found in that particular volume. Most also have a list of cases referred to in the cases reported. The important law reports are listed below, with their citations.

All England Law Reports (All ER)

Appeal Cases (AC)

Butterworth's Company Law Cases (BCLC)

British Company Cases (BCC)

Chancery Division (Ch D)

Commonwealth Law Reports (CMLR)

Criminal Appeal Reports (Cr App R)

Criminal Appeal Reports (Sentencing) (Cr App R(S))

Crown Office Digest (COD)

English Reports (ER)

Family Law (Fam Law)

Family Law Reports (FLR)

Fleet Street Reports (FSR)

Housing Law Reports (HLR)

Industrial cases Reports (ICR)

Industrial Relations Law Reports (IRLR)

Lloyd's Law Reports (Lloyd's Rep)

Probate Division (P)

Queen's Bench Division (QB)

Times Law Reports (TLR)

Weekly Law Reports (WLR)

Generally, a pamphlet will be available at the entrance to the library along with a map making it clear which law reports the library holds and where they are to be found.

iii) Legal digests

There are several very useful digests available to the legal researcher, and they generally make a useful starting point. Perhaps the best known and most useful is Halsbury's Laws of England (Butterworths), consisting of approximately 50 volumes containing the law relating to almost every subject area. The volumes are arranged alphabetically by subject and there is a general index to allow you to find the correct volume. Examples of subjects covered specifically in the volumes include injunctions, appeals, clubs, ecclesiastical law, criminal law, negligence, defamation, probate, nuisance, landlord and tenant, agency, partnership, etc. The digest will give you the relevant caselaw, the statutory law and make reference to any useful periodicals. Halsbury's is updated with loose-leaf editions produced each month and single volume supplements which appear each year.

Another useful digest is Current Law (Sweet & Maxwell), which includes the Current Law Case Citator and the Current Law Legislation Citator. The main digest, Current Law, is arranged into yearbooks with loose-leaf editions for each month of the current year. This particular digest is primarily concerned with caselaw, but also makes mention of latest statutory law, books and periodicals under general subject headings, arranged alphabetically throughout the editions, eg administrative law, contract, damages, procedure, negligence, landlord and tenant, trusts etc.

The Current Law Case Citator is very helpful. Once you do find a case you believe is particularly apt, this digest will help you to check whether or not the case has been applied, followed, distinguished or overturned in any other case. The Legislation Citator will help you find a case once you have the relevant statute or statutory instrument. More of this in later chapters.

Another digest of use to the legal researcher is the Empire & English Digest, which is arranged in volumes and subject areas in a similar way to Halsbury's Laws. However, this digest has casenotes as opposed to a commentary on the law. In this way it is somewhat less helpful than Halsbury's Laws. Halsbury's will at least attempt to explain the cases and any distinctions between them. However, the Empire and English Digest has the best cases index you will find. More of this later.

(iv) Form books

Form books are exactly what their name suggests: collections of legal documents. Practising lawyers copy and use the forms, so they do not have to reinvent the wheel every time they need a new document. The books also contain precedents for drafting which can be adapted for use by the lawyer.

Form books can be of great help if your research question involves procedure, whether civil or criminal. Judicial and administrative procedures inevitably involve the preparation and filing of forms: there are forms for almost every possible legal action, from petitioning for a divorce to changing your name, to evicting a tenant. Court rules invariably require specific documents filed in very specific formats, depending on the type of case. You can copy the format from the examples.

The documents are sometimes presented in a fill-in-the-blanks format. To accomplish a specific procedural task, the user need only choose the correct document, modify the language a little to fit the needs of the particular case, fill in the information where indicated and file the finished document in court.

Leaving nothing to chance, form books usually discuss the procedural rules that are relevant to the use of each form. In other words, when you find the form you need, chances are you will also find an overview of the procedure itself and instructions on how to make the most common modifications.

All law libraries contain some form books, most importantly Atkin's Court Forms (Butterworths) (see pages 63-64 for examples), which includes over forty volumes, and is arranged alphabetically according to subject matter. This is the mainstay of the practitioner and contains almost every type of form or pleading imaginable. It is updated regularly and refers you to the relevant court rules beneath each model form.

Of the single volume form books, the most important are:

'County Court Precedents and Pleadings' (Butterworths)

Bullen, Leake and Jacobs – 'Precedents and Pleadings' (Sweet & Maxwell)

Chitty and Jacobs – 'Queens Bench Forms' (Sweet & Maxwell) (see pages 65-66 for examples).

APPEALS TO THE COURT OF APPEAL 285

(5) FROM THE COUNTY COURT

106

NOTICE OF APPEAL: negligence[1]

IN THE COURT OF APPEAL No. ...[2]
ON APPEAL FROM [BARCHESTER] COUNTY COURT
Between A. B. ... [Plaintiff *or*
Petitioner]

and

C. D. ... [Defendant *or*
Respondent]

NOTICE OF APPEAL[3]

TAKE NOTICE that [pursuant to the leave granted by [[His *or* Her] Honour Judge .... *or* Mr[s] *or* Miss Recorder .... *or* Mr[s] *or* Miss Assistant Recorder .... *or as the case may be*[4]] *or* [the Right Honourable Lord Justice ....[5]] the Court of Appeal will be moved so soon as Counsel can be heard on behalf of the above named Plaintiff on appeal from the judgment herein of [His Honour Judge .... *or* Mr[s] Recorder .... *or* Mr[s] Assistant Recorder .... *or as the case may be*[6]] dated .... 19... whereby it was adjudged that the Plaintiff's claim should be dismissed and that judgment should be entered for the above named Defendant with costs FOR AN ORDER that the said judgment may be set aside and that judgment may be entered for the Plaintiff for the sum of £...... and the costs of the said action on scale .... to be taxed, alternatively that a new trial may be ordered AND for an order that the Defendant pay to the Plaintiff the costs of this appeal to be taxed.

AND FURTHER TAKE NOTICE that the grounds of this appeal are as follows:
1. The learned [Judge *or* Recorder *or* Assistant Recorder] misdirected himself in law in that, having found as a fact that the Plaintiff was exposed to danger and having directed himself that he must consider whether the Defendant took reasonable care for the safety of the Plaintiff, he failed properly or at all to direct himself to consider whether the Defendant had a duty in law to take steps to avoid or reduce the danger.
2. Further, and in the alternative, if the learned [Judge *or* Recorder *or* Assistant Recorder] did so direct himself, he wrongly held that in the circumstances the Defendant had no duty in law to avoid or reduce the danger.

AND FURTHER TAKE NOTICE that the Plaintiff proposes that this appeal be assigned to the County Courts (Final) List.

(Conclude and add notice as in Form 93)

1 See Table 3 Steps 52–57 ante. For the requirements of service of notice of appeal and the time limits see Paragraphs 71, 72 ante. When the notice of appeal has been served the appeal must then be set down by lodging with the Civil Appeal General Office (Room 224) the documents required by RSC Ord 59 r 5 (as substituted by RSC (Amendment No 3) 1991, SI 1991/1884); see Paragraph 73 ante. One of the copies of the notice of appeal lodged with the Civil Appeals Office on setting down must have indorsed on it a certificate of service; for a form of certificate of service see Form 94 post. The other copy of the notice of appeal must be endorsed with a receipt for the court fee; see Paragraph 73 note 10 ante.

2 Insert the county court case no.

3 The County Courts Appeals Order 1991 applies to this case and a certificate of the value of the appeal must be endorsed on the notice of appeal before it is served (RSC Ord 59 r 3A (as added by RSC (Amendment No 3) Order 1991, SI 1991/1884)); see Paragraph 69 sub-paragraph 6, particularly note 28 ante.

'Atkins Court Forms'

Form of certificate: (1) *Claims in contract, tort, monetary claims to which ibid art 2(3) applies:*
In such cases a certificate is required (unless the determination sought to be appealed from provides
for payment of a sum of money by way of debt or damages) and it should read:
    "[We [*or* I] hereby certify that the value of this appeal computed in accordance with the County
    Courts Appeals Order 1991 [exceeds *or* does not exceed] £5,000 *or* is not quantifiable]"
and the certificate must be signed by the appellant's solicitor (or the appellant, if in person).
(2) *Equity, probate cases and other proceedings to which ibid art 2(4) applies:*
In such cases a certificate of the value of the appeal is always required and it should read:
    "[We [*or* I] hereby certify that the value of this appeal computed in accordance with the County
    Courts Appeals Order 1991 [exceeds *or* does not exceed] £15,000 *or* is not quantifiable]"
and the certificate must be signed by the appellant's solicitor (or the appellant, if in person).
4 For the correct form of words to describe deputy judges, recorders and assistant recorders see note 6
    to Form 93 ante.
5 See note 4 supra.
6 See note 4 supra.

107

NOTICE OF APPEAL: committal for contempt of court[1]

(Heading as in Form 106)

NOTICE OF APPEAL

TAKE NOTICE that the Court of Appeal will be moved so soon as Counsel
can be heard on behalf of the above named Respondent on appeal from the
order of [His *or* Her] Honour Judge .... *or* Mr[s] *or* Miss Recorder
.... *or* Mr[s] or Miss Assistant Recorder .... *or as the case may be*[2]]
dated .... 19... whereby [he *or* she] sentenced the Respondent to ......
months imprisonment for contempt of court may be set aside or varied by
the substitution therefor of such punishment as may to this Honourable
Court seem fit.

AND FURTHER TAKE NOTICE that the grounds of the said appeal are as
follows:
    1. The said committal order is invalid because it does not particularise the
breaches of injunction in respect of which the order was made.
    2. [The learned [Judge *or* Recorder *or* Assistant Recorder] erred in law in
finding that the Respondent had assaulted the Petitioner in that the learned
[Judge *or* Recorder *or* Assistant Recorder] applied the civil and not the
criminal burden of proof *and/or* The finding of the learned [Judge *or* Recorder
or Assistant Recorder] was against the weight of the evidence (*give precise
details*[3]).
    3. If, contrary to the above contentions, the committal order is valid and
based upon proper findings of fact, the said sentence should have been
suspended (*give reasons why it is contended that it should have been suspended*).
    4. In the alternative, if an immediate custodial sentence was justified, the
sentence was excessive and a shorter term of imprisonment should have been
imposed.

AND FURTHER TAKE NOTICE that the Respondent proposes that this appeal
be assigned to the County Courts (Final) List.

(Conclude and add notice as in Form 93)

1 For the requirements of service of notice of appeal and the time limits see Paragraphs 71, 72 ante.
    When the notice of appeal has been served the appeal must then be set down by lodging with the
    Civil Appeal General Office (Room 224) the documents required by RSC Ord 59 r 5 (as substituted
    by RSC (Amendment No 3) 1991, SI 1991/1884); see Paragraph 73 ante. One of the copies of the
    notice of appeal lodged with the Civil Appeals Office on setting down must have indorsed on it a
    certificate of service: for a form of certificate of service see Form 94 ante. The other copy of the notice
    of appeal must be endorsed with a receipt for the court fee; see Paragraph 73 note 10 ante. The
    committal order is final (Ord 59 r 1A(5)(h)) and leave to appeal is not required. See also Vol 12 (1990
    Issue) title CONTEMPT OF COURT Paragraphs 22–26.
2 For the correct form of words to describe deputy judges, recorders and assistant recorders see note 6
    to Form 93 ante.
3 See Form 93, particularly note 13 ante.

1639 ACTION FOR POSSESSION OF LAND

1639

Summons by Plaintiff for Judgment for Possession of Land

[Title as in action]

[Formal parts as usual on application to Master] on the hearing of an application on the part of the plaintiff for final judgment in this action against the defendant *[or* the defendant *C. D.]* for possession of the land described in the statement of claim and for £— arrears of rent and mesne profits and interest thereon pursuant to section 35A of the Supreme Court Act 1981 at the rate of [   ] per cent. per annum *[or* at the rate payable on judgment debts at the date of the writ herein [and damages for breaches of covenant to be assessed and interest thereon to be assessed] and costs *[or* costs to be taxed].

Take notice that a party intending to oppose this application or to apply for a stay of execution should send to the opposite party or his solicitor, to reach him not less than three days before the date above-mentioned, a copy of any affidavit intended to be used.

Dated the —— day of—, 19—.

This summons was taken out by — of —, Solicitor for the plaintiff.

To —.

1640

Affidavit by or on Behalf of Plaintiff for Possession of Land

[Title as in action]

I, *[state name, residence, or work-place and occupation or description of deponent]* [the above-named plaintiff] make oath and say as follows:

1. I am and I was *[or* the plaintiffs are and they were] at the commencement of this action entitled to possession of the premises described in the statement of claim and the defendant is and was at the commencement of this action indebted to me [the plaintiff] in the sum of £— for arrears of rent and liable to me [the plaintiff] for mesne profits [and for damages for breaches of covenant] and interest thereon pursuant to section 35A of the Supreme Court Act 1981.

The particulars of the said claim appear by the statement of claim in this action.

2. It is within my own knowledge that I am [the plaintiffs are] entitled to possession and that the said debt and liability were incurred and are still continuing as aforesaid.

[or 2. I am informed by *[state the source of the information]* and *[or]* I verily believe *[state the grounds of belief]* that the plaintiff is entitled to

1210

Chitty & Jacobs 'Queens Bench Forms'

possession of the said premises and that the said liability was incurred and is still continuing as aforesaid.]

3. I verily believe that there is no defence to this action [save as to the amount of damages].

4. [*If not sworn by the plaintiff, add:*] I am duly authorised by the plaintiff to make this affidavit on his behalf.

Sworn [*as usual*].

This affidavit is filed on behalf of the plaintiff.

Note.—Adapted from a practice form, see PF 10.

1641

Judgment under Order 14 for Possession of Land

[*Title as in action*]

Master — in Chambers

The —— day of—, 19—.

The defendant having given notice of intention to defend and the Court having under Order 14, rule 3, ordered that judgment as hereinafter provided be entered for the plaintiff against the defendant.

It is this day adjudged that the defendant do give the plaintiff possession of the land described in the writ of summons [*or* statement of claim] as — and pay the plaintiff £— arrears of rent and £— for mesne profits at the rate of £— per annum from the —— day of—, 19—, up to the date hereof amounting in all to £— [and interest thereon at the rate of [ ] per cent. per annum *or as the case may be*] and further mesne profits at the same rate from the date hereof until possession is delivered [*or* mesne profits to be assessed] [and damages to be assessed [and for interest thereon to be assessed]] and £— costs [*or* costs to be taxed].

[*Where mesne profits or damages or interest are to be assessed, add:*]

The amount found due to the plaintiff under this judgment having been certified at £— as appears by the [Official Referee's *or* Master's Certificate *or as may be*], filed the —— day of—, 19—.

It is adjudged that the defendant do pay the plaintiff £— and costs to be taxed.

The above costs [*conclude as usual*].

Note.—This is a prescribed form, see Appendix A, No. 44.

Section 6. Relief Against Forfeiture

Chitty & Jacobs 'Queens Bench Forms'

v) Practice Manuals

Practice manuals are the bibles of the legal profession, containing as they do the relevant case and statutory law as well as very useful commentary. Many of these books are well written, well organised, and they provide detailed information on the substantive or procedural law, or both. Below is a list of the most important.

Criminal Law (substantive, procedural and evidential)

Archbold's Criminal Pleading, Evidence and Practice (Sweet & Maxwell).

This is arranged in two volumes, the first containing the law relating to procedure and evidence; the second containing the substantive law relating to criminal offences. It has cumulative supplements and regular bulletins to keep the reader up to date. It covers procedure in the Crown Court only.

Stones Justices Manual (Shaw & Sons/Butterworths)

This is arranged in three volumes and covers procedure in the Magistrates Courts only, as well as the law of evidence and the substantive law relating to summary only offences (that is, offences which can only be tried in the Magistrates Courts), and triable either - way offences (triable in the Magistrates Court or the Crown Court, at the defendant's discretion). There are copies of statutes and statutory instruments reproduced in Stones, as well as commentary on caselaw.

Civil High Court Procedure

The Supreme Court Practice (otherwise known as 'The White Book') (Sweet & Maxwell) (see page 68).

This is arranged in two volumes and a separate index, the first volume containing the Rules of the Supreme Court, with useful commentary citing cases and practice directions; the second containing forms and statutory law reproduced. There are regular supplements and bulletins to keep the reader updated.

ORDER 39

EVIDENCE BY DEPOSITION: EXAMINERS OF THE COURT

Power to order depositions to be taken (O.39, r.1)

1.—(1) The Court may, in any cause or matter where it appears necess- **39/1**
ary for the purposes of justice, make an order (in Form No.32 in Appendix
A) for the examination on oath before a Judge, an officer or examiner of
the Court or some other person at any place, of any person.

(2) An order under paragraph (1) may be made on such terms (including, in particular, terms as to the giving of discovery before the examination takes place) as the Court thinks fit and may contain an order for the
production of any document which appears to the Court to be necessary
for the purposes of the examination.

Amended by R.S.C. (Amendment) 1984 (S.I. 1984 No. 1051). Taken from former O.37.

Effect of rule 1—This is the rule under which the High Court makes its orders for the **39/1/1**
evidence to be taken in this country, before the trial, of a witness who will be unable to attend
it. The rule is, however, not limited to the taking of evidence in this country, and where it is
sought to take evidence abroad before a special examiner (*i.e.* a named individual) the order
(where the foreign law allows it) is also made under this rule. Alternatively, an order can be
made under r.2 (which applies to an examination before the British Consular Authority as
special examiner, in a convention country) or r.3 (which provides for the issue of a letter of
request—*i.e.* a request to a Court to take evidence—in any country abroad) or r.3 (which
provides for the issue of a letter of request in a convention country).

Where the circumstances render it expedient in the interests of justice to do so, the Court
has power, instead of making an order for the examination of a witness (*e.g.* an elderly lady)
under this rule, to adjourn the trial of an action under O.35, r.1, to the place where the witness is, so as to hear the oral examination of the witness as upon the trial itself (*St. Edmunds-
bury and Ipswich Diocesan Board of Finance* v. *Clark* [1973] Ch. 323; [1973] 2 All E.R. 1155). For
the practice in Admiralty actions, see O.75, r.30 and 39/2–3/8.

"In any cause or matter"—For "cause" and "matter" see S.C.A. 1981, s.151. The order
may be made by the Court in any pending proceedings (*Ex p. Hewitt* (1885) 15 Q.B.D. 159,
p.163) including matrimonial proceedings (see Family Proceedings Rules 1991, r.2.29), arbi-
trations (Arbitration Act 1950, s.12(6)(*d*)) and (in regard to evidence abroad) proceedings in
a county court (County Courts Act 1984, s.56). See also O.107, r.3.

"The Court may . . . where it appears necessary for the purposes of justice"— **39/1/2**
The exercise of the power is discretionary (see *Warner* v. *Mosses* (1880) 16 Ch.D. 100, p.102,
C.A.) but the usual grounds on which the order is made for examination in this country are
(and always have been) that the witness is too old and decrepit to attend a trial or might die
before the trial, or so ill that there is no prospect of his being able to attend the trial, or, if a
female, is pregnant and likely to be delivered about the time of the trial, or if the witness
intends to leave the country before the trial; and orders are often made in such cases by consent.

"For the examination on oath"—This includes cross-examination—for example the
cross-examination of a witness who has made an affidavit (*Concha* v. *Concha* (1886) 11 App.
Cas. 541). Or an order may be made for the examination of a witness who refuses to make an
affidavit (*Warner* v. *Mosses* (1880) 16 Ch.D. 100; *Re Springall* [1875] W.N. 225).

"Before a Judge, an officer or examiner of the Court or some other person"—The **39/1/3**
order is usually for examination before an examiner of the Court or special examiner or an
examiner agreed upon by the parties; or it can be an officer of the Court. He can, if necessary,
be supplied with the assistance of an interpreter (*Marquess of Bute* v. *James* (1886) 33 Ch.D.
157; *Baddeley* v. *Bailey* [1893] W.N. 56).

The present practice in Ch.D (contrary to the practice laid down in *Marquess of Bute* v.
James above) is to appoint a local special examiner where the evidence is to be taken outside
London. An examiner of the Court will be appointed for a hearing in London. An examination before a Judge will only be ordered in the most exceptional cases and then only with the
approval of the Judge.

A party who wishes the examination of a witness to take place before a Judge rather than
an examiner has the substantial burden of making out a sufficient case for such an order and

681

The 'White Book'

Civil County Court Procedure

The County Court Practice (otherwise known as 'The Green Book') (Butterworths) (see page 70).

This is contained in a single volume and holds the County Court Rules, relevant statutory provisions, practice directions, forms and commentary. A new edition is produced each year.

Family practice

The Family Court Practice (otherwise known as 'The Red Book') (Jordan & Sons limited)

This is contained in a single volume and contains the substantive, procedural and evidential law for this area.

vi) Practitioners' textbooks

There are available to the lawyer several specialised textbooks which are generally more detailed than student textbooks, and contain some procedural information. They will be of use to the practitioner as he or she begins their legal research. These books are considered to be good authorities and so passages contained therein can be referred to the court. The most important examples are listed below.

Agency

Bowstead - 'The Law of Agency' (Sweet & Maxwell)

Bailment

Palmer - 'Palmer on bailment ' (Sweet & Maxwell)

Civil Police Law

Clayton and Tomlinson - 'Civil Actions Against the Police' (Sweet & Maxwell)

Commercial law

Goode - 'Commercial Law' (Pelican)

NOTES TO ORDER 6, RULE 8

Address for service.—See the definition in Ord. 1, r. 3, ante, and cf. RSC Ord. 6, r. 5 (2).

Particulars settled by counsel.—Where particulars are settled by counsel, they must be signed by him and his name must appear on the copies filed by the solicitor: Ord. 50, r. 6, post.

Signature by solicitor.—The practice appears to vary, some courts insisting on an actual signature under the hand of the solicitor, whilst others accept a signature impressed by a rubber stamp. It is submitted that the latter is a sufficient compliance with the rule. What is wanted is some guarantee that the particulars have come under the personal cognisance of the solicitor or his authorised clerk.

Signature by mechanical means.—A signature may be effected, for the purpose of the rule, by the name being printed by computer or other mechanical means: see Ord. 50, r. 6A, post.

ORDER 7

SERVICE OF DOCUMENTS

PART I—GENERALLY

General mode of service

1.—(1) Where by virtue of these rules any document is required to be served on any person and no other mode of service is prescribed by any Act or rule, the document may be served—

    (a) if the person to be served is acting in person, by delivering it to him personally or by delivering it at, or sending it by first-class post to, his address for service or, if he has no address for service—

        (i) by delivering the document at his residence or by sending it by first-class post to his last known residence,

        (ii) in the case of a proprietor of a business, by delivering the document at his place of business or sending it by first-class post to his last known place of business;

    (b) if the person to be served is acting by a solicitor:—

        (i) by delivering the document at, or sending if by first-class post to, the solicitor's address for service, or

        (ii) where the solicitor's address for service includes a numbered box at a document exchange, by leaving the document at that document exchange or at a document exchange which transmits documents daily to that document exchange. [1986]

(2) In this Order "first-class post" means first-class post which has been pre-paid or in respect of which prepayment is not required.

(3) Any document which is left at a document exchange in accordance with paragraph (1) (b) (ii) shall, unless the contrary is proved, be deemed to have been served on the second day after the day on which it is left.

(4) In determining for the purposes of paragraphs (1) (b) (ii) and (3)—

    (a) whether a document exchange transmits documents daily to another document exchange, and

    (b) the second day after a document is left at a document exchange, any day on which the court office is closed shall be excluded.

NOTES TO ORDER 7, RULE 1

Scope of rule.—This rule, which may be compared with RSC Ord. 65, r. 5, lays down the general method of serving documents in county court proceedings. It is applicable wherever no other method is specifically prescribed. Thus it applies generally to the service of notice of an interlocutory application but not to the service of a summons or originating application (for which special provision is made by rr. 10 et seq., post) or to a document requiring personal service such as an order to do or abstain from doing a particular act (see Ord. 29, r. 1 (2) (a), post).

"Address for service".—This is defined in Ord. 1, r. 3, ante. An address for service must be stated in the plaintiff's particulars of claim (see Ord. 6, r. 8, ante) and in any admission, defence or counterclaim delivered by the defendant (see Ord. 9, r. 19, post). Service at the wrong address, being part of the legal process, does not give rise to an action in damages for negligence against the party instituting the proceedings: *Business Computers Ltd v Registrar of Companies* [1988] Ch 229, [1987] 3 All ER 465.

Post.—Service by post is not effected if the letter is returned undelivered: *R v County of London Quarter Sessions Appeal Committee, ex p Rossi* [1956] 1 QB 682, [1956] 1 All ER 670; *Customs and Excise Comr v Medway Draughting and Technical Services Ltd* [1989] STC 346, or where service must take place by a particular time or date and the person to be served proves that the post has not been delivered: *R v UK Central Council for Nursing Midwifery and Health Visiting, ex p Bailey* (1990)

Company law

Palmer – 'Palmer's Company Law' (Stevens & Sons)

Conflicts of law

Dicey and Morris – 'Conflicts of law' (Sweet & Maxwell)

Contract law

Chitty on Contract (Sweet & Maxwell) (two volumes)

Damages

McGregor – 'McGregor on Damages' (Sweet & Maxwell)

Family law

Rayden and Jackson – 'Divorce and Family Matters' (Butterworths)

Negligence

Charlesworth and Percy – 'Negligence' (Sweet & Maxwell)

Partnership Law

Lindley – 'Lindley on Partnership' (Sweet & Maxwell)

Professional negligence

Jackson and Powell – 'Professional Negligence' (Sweet & Maxwell)

Road traffic offences

Wilkinson – 'Road Traffic Offences' (Longman)

Torts

Clerk and Lindsell – 'The Law of Torts' (Sweet & Maxwell)

vii) Evidence manuals

Evidence is studied as a separate subject by those studying at Bar School or Law School and is an area of law which will be considered time and time again by the practitioner. The following are the main titles.

Cross – 'Cross on Evidence' (Butterworths)

Phipson – 'Phipson on Evidence' (Sweet & Maxwell)

The above titles are most likely to be used by practitioners for reference in court.

Keane – 'The Modern Law of Evidence' (Butterworths)

Murphy – 'A Practical Approach to Evidence' (Blackstone Press Ltd)

viii) Law Reviews and other legal periodicals

Because the law is always developing and changing, legal professionals are constantly analysing its evolution. There are articles about new legislation, regulations and caselaw, current legal theories and viewpoints. Law reviews and periodicals are almost always produced in paperback on a monthly or quarterly basis, and are usually bound by the librarians at the end of the year. Most law libraries will have an available list of periodicals and reviews at their entrance.

Below is a list of the more important law reviews and periodicals.

The Cambridge Law Journal (CLJ) – containing articles on all areas of the law, generally of an academic nature. It is produced quarterly.

The Criminal Law Review (Crim LR) – containing articles and the latest caselaw on substantive, procedural and evidential law, with valuable commentary.

Modern Law Review (MLR) – containing articles on all areas of the law. Produced monthly.

The Law Quarterly Review (LQR) - containing articles on all areas of law. Produced quarterly.

The Local Government Review (LGR) - containing articles in the area of administrative law, public law and local government law.

Public Law (PL) - containing articles on public and administrative law, eg judicial review.

There are many more journals which cover more specific areas of law, such as The Journal of Business Law; The Journal of Environmental Law; The Journal of Child Law, as well as the Industrial Law Journal.

There are several weekly or monthly publications often referred to as journals but are in fact 'magazines' of the legal profession. They are useful for the most up-to-date information on many different areas of the law. The majority of the articles they contain are concerned with the practical aspects of the law. The most important are listed below.

'Counsel' - the monthly magazine for barristers, produced by the Bar Council.

'Estates Gazette' (EG) - produced weekly and contains articles on the areas of planning and land law.

'The Law Society Gazette' (LSG) - produced weekly by the solicitors profession, and contains articles on all areas.

'New Law Journal' (NLJ) - produced weekly, containing articles on all areas as well as casenotes.

'Solicitors' Journal' (SJ) - produced weekly, with articles on all areas.

In order to find the relevant article or articles which may help you in your quest for the answer, an important publication is the 'Legal Journals Index', which is published quarterly and contains a subject index. Look up your subject in the index and you will be referred to a number of articles on the point. The publication also has a

legislation index and a caselaw index which enable you to find articles when you already have a relevant case or know the relevant statutory law (see page 74). Many law libraries also have a legal journals index on computer (see later chapters).

Current Law (referred to earlier) lists relevant articles under each of its subject headings.

ix) Specialised loose-leaf publications

Most practising lawyers and many others who work in the legal system, such as teachers, legal executives, legal research specialists and even some law librarians, find it necessary to specialise. There is just too much information generated by the courts and legislatures to keep up on everything. Specialisation typically means not only mastering a particular body of knowledge—for example, tax, planning, bankruptcy or personal injury— but keeping on top of it.

Several publications cater to this need by offering an exhaustive loose-leaf compilation of recent developments in a certain field and weekly or monthly loose-leaf supplements. These materials provide information about new laws, regulations, and judicial and administrative decisions that might affect the field of law covered by the publication.

For anyone who must maintain an up-to-the-minute grasp on what is going on in a particular legal area, these services can prove invaluable. However, they may be too specialised for your purposes unless your research topic falls squarely within one of these special categories. If it does, locate the appropriate service, read the instructions on how to use it at the front of the first volume and check the index. You may solve your problem almost immediately. All the loose-leaf services listed below can be found in a good law library.

Examples of loose-leaf publications include a variety of Butterworths' services on:

Company law - 'Company Law Service'

Family law - 'Family Law Service'

Immigration law – 'Immigration Law Service'

Personal injury litigation – 'Personal Injury Litigation Service'

Road Traffic Offences – 'Road Traffic Service'
    Others include:

Air Law

Shawcross and Beaumont – 'Air Law'

Child law

Clarke, Hall and Morrison – 'Clarke, Hall and Morrison on Children' (Butterworths)

Company law

Palmer – 'Company Law' (Sweet & Maxwell)

Education

'The Law of Education' (Butterworths)

Employment law

Harvey – 'Industrial Relations and Employment Law' (Butterworths)

Food and Drugs

'Butterworths' Law of Food and Drugs'

Landlord and Tenant

Hill and Redman – 'Hill and Redman's Law of Landlord and Tenant' (Butterworths)

Woodfall – 'Landlord and Tenant' (Sweet & Maxwell)

Quantum of damages in personal injury cases

Kemp & Kemp – 'The Quantum of Damages' (Sweet & Maxwell)

(See also the Current Law Yearbooks and monthly editions for quantum in personal injury cases)

Tax Law

The British Tax Encyclopaedia (Sweet & Maxwell)

'Simon's Taxes Encyclopaedia'

REVIEW

Questions

1   What is the primary reason for using background resources to start your research?

2   What are law student texts most useful for?

3   What are the advantages of starting your legal research in a legal Encyclopaedia?

4   When can legal periodicals be of use to the legal researcher?

5   How can you find articles of interest in legal periodicals and law reviews?

Answers

1   To get a general understanding of the relevant legal area before looking for the specific answer to a narrow question. The answers to almost all specific legal questions depend on a number of variables which the background resource can alert you to.

2   These books, which are conceptual in nature, are excellent if you want a basic understanding of the variables in any specific area of concern. Some of the more detailed textbooks can be of use to the practitioner, especially those on the subjects of criminal and civil procedure and evidence. The practitioner should not reject them all out of hand.

3   Legal Encyclopaedias cover the entire range of the law for a particular subject area; for example, employment law, landlord and tenant, consumer credit law, environmental health law, financial services law, and foods and drugs. The Encyclopaedias are broken down into small segments, making it easier for you to find the law relating to your particular question. Each segment will refer you to cases, periodicals, and statutory law, with useful

commentary added. Often, the Encyclopaedias will reproduce the relevant statutes in an appendix. They are a good starting point for your moving on to more detailed research.

4 When you are interested in new legislation, new caselaw and innovative legal theories. You will also find useful articles disseminating a long line of caselaw. Also, articles of particular use to practitioners can often be found, dealing with such things as recent changes to rules of court and practice directions.

5 The Legal Journals Index on computer or in paperback is a very comprehensive and useful publication, with a legislation, subject and caseindex to give you as much chance as possible to find the most useful articles for your research area. Current Law will also point you to articles in its yearbook and monthly editions – under its different subject sections.

Chapter 6

Statutes, Statutory Instruments, Regulations and By-laws

A   Introduction to Statutes

When your legal research problem may include consideration of statutory law it is vitally important to look at that law first before moving straight onto the caselaw which interprets or applies it. There are several publications which reproduce complete statutes, with brief commentary and explanation underneath. The two most useful are Halsbury's Statutes (Butterworths) (see pages 84-85), organised in volumes according to subject matter and Current Law Statutes Annotated (Sweet & Maxwell), organised in volumes according to the year of the statute.

B   How to Find Statutes

1   Using background materials

If you do not know which statute it is you are looking for to help you answer your legal research question, or if you are unaware of whether or not any statutory law applies, you will find it easiest to look first at a background resource, eg textbook or encyclopaedia, and determine which particular statute is the relevant one. It is vitally important to ensure that you have the correct statute in mind. This means considering when the statute is meant to apply. For example, in the Criminal Justice Act 1991 it is made clear that its provisions should not apply where the criminal offence took place before the statute came into force - ie 1 October 1992. If the offence you are considering took place before that time then you have to look at the common law and the Powers Of Criminal Courts Act 1973; if after, then you must consider the provisions of the Criminal Justice Act 1991.

It is extremely important then, that each and every time, you determine which is the applicable statute - by considering what is the important incident which determines this. For example, with some statutes the determining factor may be the date the contracts were exchanged, and the statute may not apply to contracts exchanged before the date the statute came into force.

Members of principal councils

3 Chairman

(1) The chairman of a principal council shall be elected annually by the council from among the councillors.

(2) The chairman shall, unless he resigns or becomes disqualified, continue in office until his successor becomes entitled to act as chairman.

(3) During his term of office the chairman shall continue to be a member of the council notwithstanding the provisions of this Act relating to the retirement of councillors.

(4) The chairman of a district council shall have precedence in the district, but not so as prejudicially to affect Her Majesty's royal prerogative.

(5) A principal council may pay the chairman for the purpose of enabling him to meet the expenses of his office such allowance as the council think reasonable.

NOTES

Principal council. Ie a council elected for a non-metropolitan county or a district; see s 270(1) post, as read with s 8(1) post.

Shall be elected annually. See, further, s 4 post.

Disqualified. As to the disqualification for membership of a local authority, see ss 80, 81 post.

Shall continue to be a member. A person who is treated as continuing to be a member by virtue of sub-s (3) above is disregarded for the purposes of "membership" in relation to the Local Government and Housing Act 1989, ss 15–17, Sch 1 (political balance on committees, etc); see s 15 of, and Sch 1, para 4(1) to, that Act post, as from a day to be appointed under s 195(2) thereof.

Provisions of this Act relating to the retirement of councillors. See, in particular, s 7 post.

District council. As to the districts in England and their councils, see ss 1(1), (3), (4), 2(2), (3) ante, Sch 1, Pt I, Sch 3, para 1 post.

Greater London. This section does not apply; see s 8(1) post.

4 Election of chairman

(1) The election of the chairman shall be the first business transacted at the annual meeting of a principal council.

(2) If, apart from section 3(3) above or section 5(2) below, the person presiding at the meeting would have ceased to be a member of the council, he shall not be entitled to vote in the election except in accordance with subsection (3) below.

(3) In the case of an equality of votes the person presiding at the meeting shall give a casting vote in addition to any other vote he may have.

NOTES

Annual meeting. Such a meeting is required by s 99, Sch 12, Pt I, para 1 post.

Principal council. Ie a council elected for a non-metropolitan county or a district; see s 270(1) post, as read with s 8(1) post.

Greater London. This section does not apply; see s 8(1) post.

5 Vice-chairman

(1) A principal council shall appoint a member of the council to be vice-chairman of the council.

(2) The vice-chairman shall, unless he resigns or becomes disqualified, hold office until immediately after the election of a chairman at the next annual meeting of the council and during that time shall continue to be a member of the council notwithstanding the provisions of this Act relating to the retirement of councillors.

LOCAL GOVERNMENT ACT 1972 s 6   **179**

(3) Subject to any standing orders made by the council, anything authorised or required to be done by, to or before the chairman may be done by, to or before the vice-chairman.

(4) A principal council may pay the vice-chairman for the purpose of enabling him to meet the expenses of his office such allowance as the council think reasonable.

NOTES

Principal council. Ie a council elected for a non-metropolitan county or a district; see s 270(1) post, as read with s 8(1) post.
Disqualified. As to disqualification for membership of a local authority, see ss 80, 81 post.
Annual meeting. Such a meeting is required by s 99, Sch 12, Pt I, para 1 post.
Provisions of this Act relating to the retirement of councillors. See, in particular, s 7 post.
Greater London. This section does not apply; see s 8(1) post.

6 Term of office and retirement of councillors

(1) Councillors for a principal area shall be elected by the local government electors for that area in accordance with this Act and Part I of the [Representation of the People Act 1983].

(2) For the purposes of the election of councillors—

    (*a*) every [non-metropolitan] county shall be divided into electoral divisions, each returning (subject to paragraph 3 of Schedule 3 to this Act) one councillor;

    (*b*) every metropolitan district shall be divided into wards, each returning a number of councillors which is divisible by three; and

    (*c*) every non-metropolitan district shall be divided into wards, each returning such number of councillors as may be provided by an order under the said paragraph 3 or under or by virtue of the provisions of section 7 below or Part IV of this Act;

and there shall be a separate election for each electoral division or ward.

NOTES

The words in square brackets in sub-s (1) were substituted by the Representation of the People Act 1983, s 206, Sch 8, para 12, and the words in square brackets in sub-s (2)(*a*) were inserted by the Local Government Act 1985, s 102(1), Sch 16, para 2. It will be observed that the marginal note to this section does not correctly indicate its subject-matter.
Elected . . . in accordance with this Act. See s 7 post and, as to qualifications and disqualifications for membership of local authorities, ss 79–81 post. The registration of electors and conduct of elections was originally governed by Pt III (ss 39–45) (repealed) of this Act, but is now governed by provisions of the Representation of the People Act 1983, Pt I, Vol 15, title Elections, which replaced the provisions of the said Pt III.
Non-metropolitan county. As to the non-metropolitan counties in England and their councils, see ss 1(1), (2), 2(1), (3) ante, and Sch 1, Pt II post. The councils of the metropolitan counties (see Sch 1, Pt I post) were abolished on 1 April 1986 by the Local Government Act 1985, s 1 post.
Metropolitan district. As to the metropolitan districts in England and their councils, see ss 1(1), (3), 2(2), (3) ante, and Sch 1, Pt I, col 2 post.
Non-metropolitan district. As to the non-metropolitan districts in England and their councils, see ss 1(1), (4), 2(2), (3) ante, and Sch 3, para 1 post.
Pt IV of this Act. Ie ss 46–78 post.
Greater London. This section does not apply; see s 8(1) post.
Definitions. For "non-metropolitan county" and "non-metropolitan district", see s 270(2) post; for "principal area", see s 270(1) post, with s 8(1) post.
Representation of the People Act 1983, Part I. See Vol 15, title Elections.

Once you have determined which is the relevant statute, you should use the index of one of the above-mentioned publications (Halsbury's or Current Law) to find the statute you want to consider. The indexes are arranged both by the years of the statutes and alphabetically, so that you can easily find the statute even if you only have its year or only its name. Check the contents list to the statute at the front and ensure you read all relevant sections before turning to the particular section you think is relevant. If a statutory instrument or code has been made under the relevant sections of the statute, then read them also (for which see later in this chapter).

An alternative is to look at one of the various encyclopaedias listed earlier. Each generally has an appendix which contains all relevant statutes for the law subject the encyclopaedia covers. Butterworths also produces various books which only reproduce statutes and statutory instruments. For example Butterworth's Insolvency Law Handbook; Butterworth's Road Traffic Law; Butterworth's Employment Law Handbook; Butterworth's Company Law Handbook; and Butterworth's Landlord and Tenant Handbook.

2 Using cases to find statutes

If you cannot find a relevant background resource, but are aware of a relevant case, look at the report of the case and you will see the statutory law considered by the court cited after the headnotes. Once you have the name of the statute use Halsbury's or Current Law to look at the complete statute – it is not advisable just to rely on the small section of the statute which may be quoted in the report.

3 Using digests to find statutes

If you are unable to find a relevant background resource, perhaps because the question concerns a general area which covers almost all areas of law, eg friendly societies; and you are not in possession of a relevant case, then it would be useful to use digests which should tell you about the statutory law. For example, look at the 'Friendly Societies' section in the relevant volume of Halsbury's Laws and the statutory law will be referred to in the main text or the notes to it. Then turn to Halsbury's Statutes or Current Law Statutes Annotated to look at the full text of the statute.

4 Using other indexes to find statutes

Some law libraries have computer indexes which will refer you to relevant statutory law when you enter a subject area into it. For more on this, see Chapter 12.

C How to Find Recent or Pending Legislation

In order to find recent legislation which you have been referred to, or in order to check that the statute or section you have already looked at is the most recent and therefore still in force, look at the monthly updates produced for Halsbury's Statutes. These are usually to be found in a loose-leaf file on the same shelves as the volumes. Check that you have considered the latest monthly edition. They will tell you of any recent legislation and its effect on any other statutes - ie if it has amended or repealed any older statutes.

Alternatively, check the monthly updates produced for Halsbury's Laws. These are also to be found in a loose-leaf file on the same shelves as Halsbury's Laws. Ensure that you know the subject name and, preferably, the paragraph numbers which cover your problem in the main volumes - the updates are organised in this way. Again, ensure that you have considered the latest update. The text should tell you of any legislation which has just been passed by Parliament, and any legislation which has just come into force and its effect on any earlier legislation.

The Current Law monthly editions, organised by subject index, will also refer to any legislation which has just been passed or which has just come into force.

Another possibility is to check the magazines produced by the legal profession, such as the New Law Journal or The Law Society Gazette, which come out each week. Consider also the weekly news bulletins produced by The Supreme Court Practice and Archbold's

D   How to Discover if the Statute is in Force

You may have been referred to a statute or section, and you may wonder whether it has since been repealed by other later legislation. You may also have been referred to a statute which has been passed by Parliament, but you are unsure whether it is in force yet. Obviously it is vitally important that you find out the answer to these questions.

The easiest way to discover the answer is to look at the volumes of Halsbury's Statutes named, 'Is It In Force?' (see pages 89–90). These are loose-leaf volumes to be found on the same shelves as Halsbury's Statutes. An alternative approach is to consider the publications mentioned at C (above).

Whenever you need to check when a statute came into force, you need to find the section or schedule of the statute which deals with commencement or find the relevant page in 'Is it in Force?' These will usually refer you to a statutory instrument which will give the exact date of commencement. Unfortunately, it is generally the case that different sections of the statute come into force at different times. This means the statute will often refer you to many different statutory instruments. As for finding these statutory instruments, see later in this chapter.

E   How to Find Out-of-Date Statutes

If the most recent legislation does not apply to your research problem because, for example, the incident giving rise to the litigation occurred before that legislation came into force, then you will need to consider the provisions of the statutory law which were in force at the relevant time, but are now repealed. If the legislation in force at the relevant time was repealed by the present legislation, then the new statute will mention it.

If you want to look at the old statute do not use Halsbury's Statutes as it only reproduces current legislation. You should look at Current Law Statutes Annotated instead – the volume for the year of the repealed statute. Law libraries tend not to keep out-of-date textbooks and so the commentary in Current Law on the old statute may be of vital importance.

534	1990

Enterprise and New Towns (Scotland) Act 1990 (c 35)—*cont*

s 21(1)–(3)	1 Apr 1991 (SI 1990/1840)
(4)	1 Oct 1990 (SI 1990/1840)
22	1 Oct 1990 (SI 1990/1840)
23(1)–(3)	1 Apr 1991 (SI 1990/1840)
(4)	See Sch 3 below
24	1 Apr 1991 (SI 1990/1840)
25(1)	See Sch 2 below
(2)–(4)	1 Apr 1991 (SI 1990/1840)
26(1), (2)	1 Oct 1990 (SI 1990/1840)
(3), (4)	1 Apr 1991 (SI 1990/1840)
27	1 Oct 1990 (SI 1990/1840)
28	1 Apr 1991 (SI 1990/1840)
29, 30	1 Oct 1990 (SI 1990/1840)
31, 32	1 Apr 1991 (SI 1990/1840)
33–35	1 Oct 1990 (SI 1990/1840)
36, 37	26 Jul 1990 (s 39(1), (3))
38(1)	See Sch 4 below
(2)	See Sch 5 below
(3), (4)	1 Apr 1991 (SI 1990/1840)
39	26 Jul 1990 (RA)
40	1 Apr 1991 (SI 1990/1840)
Sch 1	1 Oct 1990 (SI 1990/1840)
2, para 1	1 Oct 1990 (SI 1990/1840)
2–6	1 Apr 1991 (SI 1990/1840)
3, para 1–3	1 Apr 1991 (SI 1990/1840)
4, 5	26 Jul 1990 (s 39(1), (3))
6–9	1 Apr 1991 (SI 1990/1840)
4, para 1	1 Oct 1990 (SI 1990/1840)
2–5	1 Apr 1991 (SI 1990/1840)
6	1 Oct 1990 (SI 1990/1840)
7–18	1 Apr 1991 (SI 1990/1840)
5	26 Jul 1990 (s 39(1), (3))

Entertainments (Increased Penalties) Act 1990 (c 20)

RA: 13 Jul 1990

13 Jul 1990 (RA)

Environmental Protection Act 1990 (c 43)

RA: 1 Nov 1990

Commencement provisions: s 164(2), (3); Environmental Protection Act 1990 (Commencement No 1) Order 1990, SI 1990/2226; Environmental Protection Act 1990 (Commencement No 2) Order 1990, SI 1990/2243; Environmental Protection Act 1990 (Commencement No 3) Order 1990, SI 1990/2565; Environmental Protection Act 1990 (Commencement No 4) Order 1990, SI 1990/2635 (also amends SI 1990/2565); Environmental Protection Act 1990 (Commencement No 5) Order 1991, SI 1991/96; Environmental Protection Act 1990 (Commencement No 6 and Appointed Day) Order 1991, SI 1991/685; Environmental Protection Act 1990 (Commencement No 7) Order 1991, SI 1991/1042; Environmental Protection Act 1990 (Commencement No 8) Order 1991, SI 1991/1319; Environmental Protection Act 1990 (Commencement No 9) Order 1991, SI 1991/1577; Environmental Protection Act 1990 (Commencement

Halsbury's 'Is it in Force?'

For example, section 21(4) of the Enterprise and New Towns (Scotland) Act 1990 came into force on 1 October 1990, pursuant to S.I. No. 1840 of 1990.

1990   **535**

Environmental Protection Act 1990 (c 43)—*cont*
No 10) Order 1991, SI 1991/2829; Environmental Protection Act 1990
(Commencement No 11) Order 1992, SI 1992/266; Environmental Protection
Act 1990 (Commencement No 12) Order 1992, SI 1992/3253

s 1, 2	1 Jan 1991 (SI 1990/2635)
3	19 Dec 1991 (SI 1990/2635)
4, 5	1 Jan 1991 (SI 1990/2635)
6	See Sch 1 below
7–28	1 Jan 1991 (SI 1990/2635)
29–31	31 May 1991 (SI 1991/1319)
32	See Sch 2 below
33(1)(a), (b)	*Not in force*
(c)	1 Apr 1992 (SI 1991/2829)
(2)	1 Apr 1992 (so far as relates to s 33(1)(c)) (SI 1991/2829)
	Not in force (otherwise)
(3), (4)	13 Dec 1991 (SI 1991/2829)
(5)	*Not in force*
(6)–(9)	1 Apr 1992 (so far as relates to s 33(1)(c)) (SI 1991/2829)
	Not in force (otherwise)
34(1)–(4)	1 Apr 1992 (SI 1991/2829)
(5)	13 Dec 1991 (SI 1991/2829)
(6)	1 Apr 1992 (SI 1991/2829)
(7)–(9)	13 Dec 1991 (SI 1991/2829)
(10)	1 Apr 1992 (SI 1991/2829)
(11)	13 Dec 1991 (SI 1991/2829)
35–44	*Not in force*
45(1)	14 Feb 1992 (so far as enables orders or regulations to be made) (SI 1992/266)
	1 Apr 1992 (otherwise) (SI 1992/266)
(2)	14 Feb 1992 (so far as enables orders or regulations to be made) (SI 1992/266)
	1 Apr 1992 (otherwise) (S) (SI 1992/266)
	Not in force (otherwise) (EW)
(3)–(12)	14 Feb 1992 (so far as enable orders or regulations to be made) (SI 1992/266)
	1 Apr 1992 (otherwise) (SI 1992/266)
46, 47	1 Apr 1992 (SI 1992/266)
48(1)–(6)	1 Apr 1992 (SI 1992/266)
(7)	*Not in force*
(8), (9)	1 Apr 1992 (SI 1992/266)
49	1 Aug 1991 (SI 1991/1577)
50, 51	31 May 1991 (SI 1991/1319)
52(1)	1 Apr 1992 (SI 1992/266)
(2)	*Not in force*
(3)–(7)	1 Apr 1992 (SI 1992/266)
(8)	13 Dec 1991 (so far as relates to s 52(1), (3)) (SI 1991/2829)
	Not in force (otherwise)
(9)–(11)	1 Apr 1992 (SI 1992/266)
53	1 Apr 1992 (SI 1992/266)
54	*Not in force*
55, 56	1 Apr 1992 (SI 1992/266)
57–59	*Not in force*
60	31 May 1991 (so far as relates to anything deposited at a place for the deposit of waste, or in a

If all you have is the date the incident took place which gave rise to the litigation then the easiest thing to do is to check the latest statute which will tell you the statute it repealed. If the repealed statute was brought into force after the incident then you will have to find the repealed statute in Current Law Statutes Annotated and see from that which statute it repealed. Keep doing this until you find the right statute. In order to determine when any of these statutes came into force, follow the same procedure as mentioned above at D, in relation to statutory instruments.

F How to Read Statutes

Most legal research projects involve finding out what the law 'is' in a particular circumstance. This usually involves finding a statute and then deciding how a court would interpret it given the facts in your situation. Courts consider it their responsibility to carry out the legislature's will as expressed in its statutes. If a statute is unclear—and many are—the court will try to determine what the legislature intended.

From the time a proposed statute is drafted until it emerges from the legislature in final form, legislators compromise, delete words and add more words in an attempt to get enough votes to pass the bill. What may have begun as straightforward and clear language often becomes so riddled with exceptions and conditions that the result presents serious difficulties to anyone who wants to understand what was intended.

When searching for the meaning of a statutory provision, courts employ a number of rules of interpretation that have been developed over the years. These 'rules' are often imprecise and sometimes contradictory, but if you are aware of them you should arrive at a more accurate interpretation than if you use only your common sense. Below are some guidelines that reflect the approach used by the courts for reading and understanding statutes.

Rule 1: Read the statute at least three times. Then read it again

Often a different and hopefully more accurate meaning will emerge from each reading. Never feel that somehow you are inadequate because despite a number of readings you are not sure what a particular statute means. A great many lawsuits result from the fact that lawyers disagree about confusing statutory language.

Rule 2: Pay close attention to 'ands' and 'ors'

Many statutes have lots of 'ands' and 'ors' tucked into different clauses, and the thrust of the statute often depends on which clauses are joined by an 'and' and which by an 'or'. When clauses are joined by an 'or', it means that the conditions in at least one of the clauses must be present but not in all. When clauses are joined by an 'and', the conditions in all the clauses must be met.

Rule 3: Assume all words and punctuation in the statute have meaning

Often, statutes seem to be internally inconsistent or redundant. Sometimes they are. However, courts presume that every word and comma in a statute means something, and you should do the same. If you are unsure about what a word or phrase mans, look it up in a law dictionary or the multi-volume publication titled Words and Phrases. (See section H below for a discussion of this resource.)

Rule 4: Interpret a statute so that it is consistent with all other related statutes, if possible

Sometimes it appears that a statute is totally inconsistent with other statutes in the same statutory scheme. It may be, but a judge who examines the statutes will make an attempt to reconcile the meanings so that no conflict exists. It is wise, therefore, to ask yourself whether any interpretation of the statute can be made which will make it consistent rather than inconsistent with other statutes.

Rule 5: Interpret the statute so that it makes sense and does not lead to absurd or improbable results

Courts are sometimes called on to interpret statutes that, if taken literally, would lead to a result that the legislature could not (in the court's opinion) have intended. In such an instance, a court will strain to interpret the statute so that it does make sense or lead to a logical result.

Rule 6: Track down all cross-references to other statutes and sections

People who draft statutes are very fond of including references to other statutes and sections of the same statute. When faced with such a statute, the human tendency is to ignore the cross-references and hope that they don't pertain to your situation. It would be advisable, quite simply, to track down each and every cross-reference and make sure you understand how it relates to the main body of the statute you are analysing. If you do not, you could overlook something crucial.

G   The Importance of Cases which Interpret Statutes

Statutes are subject to varying degrees of interpretation, no matter how clear they appear to be. Therefore, it is very important that you do not end your research with the reading of the statute alone. There are two basic ways in which you can find the cases that interpret the statute in question:

i)   Check the notes accompanying the statutes reproduced in the annotated volumes of Halsbury's or Current Law Statutes Annotated.

ii)   Check the Current Law Legislation Citator (see pages 94–95), usually published once a year. Its index lists all statutes and statutory instruments, and refers you to cases which have cited that legislation in the year(s) the publication is concerned with.

CAP.

1971—cont.

78. Town and Country Planning Act 1971—cont.
  s. 246, see *Strandmill v. Secretary of State for the Environment; South Buckinghamshire District Council v. Secretary of State for the Environment* [1988] 2 P.L.R. 1; *Marder Q.C.; White v. Secretary of State for the Environment* [1989] 15 E.G. 193, C.A.; *F.G. Whitley & Sons v. Secretary of State for Wales, The Times,* October 24, 1989, Layfield Q.C.; *Young v. Secretary of State for the Environment, The Times,* February 26, 1990, C.A.
  s. 277, see *Westminster City Council v. Secretary of State for the Environment* [1988] 3 P.L.R. 104, Spence Q.C.; *Steinberg and Sykes v. Secretary of State for the Environment and Camden London Borough Council* [1989] J.P.L. 258, Lionel Read Q.C.; *Ward v. Secretary of State for the Environment, The Times,* October 5, 1989, C.A.; *Harrow London Borough Council v. Secretary of State for the Environment, The Times,* December 15, 1989, D.C.; *Save Britain's Heritage v. Secretary of State for the Environment, The Times,* April 4, 1990, C.A.
  s. 277A, regs. 90/1147.
  s. 287, regs. 89/603, 670, 1087; 90/881, 1147; orders 88/2091; 89/1590, 2454; 90/457, 465.
  s. 290, see *R. v. Leominster District Council, ex p. Antique Country Buildings* (1988) 56 P. & C.R. 240, Mann J.
  s. 290, regs. 89/1087; 90/1147.
  s. 290, amended: 1989, c.15, sch.25; order 90/776; repealed in pt.: 1989, c.29, sch.18.
  sch. 8, see *Richmond Gateways v. Richmond upon Thames London Borough Council* [1989] 29 R.V.R. 78, C.A.; *Camden London Borough Council v. ADC Estates, The Times,* June 27, 1990, C.A.
  sch. 9, see *Hertsmere Borough Council v. Mattock* (1988) 3 P.A.D. 378; *Wigan Metropolitan Borough Council v. Nicholson* (1988) 3 P.A.D. 400; *Bolsover District Council v. Sengupta* (1988) 3 P.A.D. 404.
  sch. 9, regs. 89/1087.
  schs. 11, 21, regs. 90/1147.
  sch. 23, repealed in pt.: 1989, c.42, sch.12.
  sch. 24, see *Colley v. Canterbury City Council* [1989] J.P.L. 532, Millett J.
80. Banking and Financial Dealings Act 1971.
  ss. 4, 5, repealed in pt.: 1989, c.38, sch.7.

1972

5. Local Employment Act 1972.
  sch. 3, repealed in pt.: 1990, c.11, sch.1.
6. Summer Time Act 1972.
  s. 2, order 89/985.
7. Civil List Act 1972.
  ss. 1–3, amended: order 90/2018.
  s. 6, order 90/2018.
11. Superannuation Act 1972.
  s. 1, orders 89/1874; 90/757.
  s. 1, amended: 1990, c.7, s.8.
  s. 2, amended: *ibid.,* s.9.
  s. 7, regs. 89/371, 372, 802(S.), 967(S.); 90/422(S.), 503, 521, 1284(S.), 1709.
  ss. 9, regs. 89/378, 666(S.), 808(S.), 811, 946; 90/383(S.).

CAP.

1972—cont.

11. Superannuation Act 1972—cont.
  s. 9, amended: 1990, c.7, ss.4, 8, 11.
  s. 10, regs. 89/804, 807(S.), 1749(S.); 90/382(S.).
  s. 10, amended: 1990, c.7, ss.4, 8.
  s. 12, regs. 89/371, 372, 378, 666(S.), 802(S.), 804, 807(S.), 808(S.), 946, 967(S.), 1462, 1624, 1749(S.); 90/382(S.), 383(S.), 442(S.), 521, 1284(S.), 1709, 1841.
  s. 16, order 90/1841.
  s. 19, repealed: S.L.R. 1989.
  s. 24, regs. 89/298, 1139; 90/125(S.), 1433.
  sch. 1, amended: order 90/757.
  sch. 3, regs. 89/804, 811.
  schs. 4, 6, repealed in pt.: S.L.R. 1989.
17. Electricity Act 1972.
  repealed: 1989, c.29, sch.18.
18. Maintenance Orders (Reciprocal Enforcement) Act 1972.
  ss. 28, 28A, amended: 1990, c.41, sch.16.
  s. 30, repealed in pt.: *ibid.,* schs.16, 20.
  s. 41, repealed: 1989, c.41, sch.15.
20. Road Traffic Act 1972.
  see *D.P.P. v. Porthouse* [1989] R.T.R. 177, D.C.; *D.P.P. v. Yates* [1989] R.T.R. 134, D.C.
  s. 1, see *McCluskey v. H.M. Advocate,* 1989 S.L.T. 175; *R. v. Griffiths* (1989) 88 Cr.App.R. 6, C.A.; *R. v. Rodenhouse, The Times,* May 11, 1989, C.A.; *Crowe v. H.M. Advocate,* 1989 S.C.C.R. 681; *Att.-Gen.'s References (Nos. 3 and 5 of 1989)* [1989] R.T.R. 337, C.A.; *R. v. Clarke* (1990) 91 Cr.App.R. 69, C.A.; *R. v. Lamb (Charles)* (1990) 91 Cr.App.R. 181, C.A.
  s. 2, see *R. v. Conway* [1988] 3 W.L.R. 1238, C.A.; *McNab v. Guild,* 1989 S.C.C.R. 138, *Smith v. Wilson,* 1989 S.C.C.R. 395.
  s. 3, see *Malpas v. Hamilton,* 1988 S.C.C.R. 546; *McCrone v. Normand,* 1989 S.L.T. 332; *D.P.P. v. Parker* [1989] R.T.R. 413, D.C.; *MacPhail v. Haddow,* 1990 S.C.C.R. 339.
  s. 5, see *Cole v. D.P.P.* [1988] R.T.R. 224, D.C.; *D.P.P. v. Webb* [1988] R.T.R. 374, D.C.; *D.P.P. v. Watkins* [1989] 1 All E.R. 1126, D.C.; *Gardner v. D.P.P.* [1989] R.T.R. 384, D.C.; *MacPherson v. Ingram,* 1990 S.C.C.R. 452.
  s. 6, see *Askew v. D.P.P.* [1988] R.T.R. 303, D.C.; *Gumbley v. Cunningham* [1989] 2 W.L.R. 1, H.L.; *D.P.P. v. Feeney, The Times,* December 13, 1988, D.C.; *Smith v. D.P.P., The Times,* February 16, 1989, D.C.; *McLeod v. MacDougall,* 1989 S.L.T. 151; *Garner v. D.P.P., The Times,* April 17, 1989, D.C.; *D.P.P. v. O'Meara* [1989] R.T.R. 24, D.C.; *D.P.P. v. Frost* [1989] R.T.R. 11, D.C.; *Hassan v. Scott,* 1989 S.L.T. 380; *Hodgkins v. Carmichael,* 1989 S.C.C.R. 69; *Beauchamp-Thompson v. D.P.P.* [1989] R.T.R. 54, D.C.; *D.P.P. v. Watkins* [1989] 1 All E.R. 1126, D.C.; *D.P.P. v. Parkin* [1989] Crim.L.R. 379, D.C.; *McArthur v. Valentine,* 1989 S.C.C.R. 704; *Giordano v. Carmichael,* 1990 S.C.C.R. 61; *Oswald v. D.P.P.* [1989] R.T.R. 360, D.C.; *D.P.P. v. Jones* [1990] R.T.R. 33, D.C.; *Regan v. D.P.P.* [1989] Crim.L.R. 832, D.C.; *Smith v. D.P.P.* [1990] R.T.R. 17, D.C.; *D.P.P. v. Younas* [1990] R.T.R. 22, D.C.; *D.P.P. v. Barker* [1990] R.T.R. 1, D.C.; *Gardner v. D.P.P.* [1989] R.T.R. 384, D.C.; *D.P.P. v. Gordon, D.P.P. v. Griggs* [1990] R.T.R. 71, D.C.

STATUTE CITATOR 1989–90   **1972**

CAP.

1972—cont.

20. Road Traffic Act 1972—cont.

s. 7, see *Askew* v. *D.P.P.* [1988] R.T.R. 303, D.C; *Grady* v. *Pollard* [1988] R.T.R. 316, D.C.; *Cole* v. *D.P.P.* [1988] R.T.R. 224, D.C.; *Gardner* v. *D.P.P.* [1989] R.T.R. 384, D.C.

s. 8, see *Askew* v. *D.P.P.* [1988] R.T.R. 303, D.C.; *Grady* v. *Pollard* [1988] R.T.R. 316, D.C.; *Cole* v. *D.P.P.* [1988] R.T.R. 224, D.C.; *D.P.P.* v. *Fountain* [1988] R.T.R. 385, D.C.; *D.P.P.* v. *Magill* [1988] R.T.R. 337, D.C.; *R.* v. *Waltham Forest Justices, ex p. Barton, The Times,* April 19, 1989, D.C.; *D.P.P.* v. *Frost* [1989] R.T.R. 11, D.C.; *Gallacher* v. *Scott,* 1989 S.L.T. 397; *Hamilton* v. *Jones* (Sh.Ct.), 1989 S.C.C.R. 1; *Hodgkins* v. *Carmichael,* 1989 S.C.C.R. 69; *Jamsheed* v. *Walkingshaw,* 1989 S.C.C.R. 75; *Wyllie* v. *Crown Prosecution Service* (1988) Crim.L.R. 753, D.C.; *Lockhart* v. *Stanbridge,* 1989 S.C.C.R. 220; *Smith* v. *D.P.P.* [1989] R.T.R. 159, D.C.; *McCIroy* v. *Owen-Thomas,* 1989 S.C.C.R. 402; *McGuinness* v. *Jessop,* 1989 S.C.C.R. 349; *D.P.P.* v. *Parkin* [1989] Crim.L.R. 379, D.C.; *Regan* v. *D.P.P., The Times,* September 2, 1989, D.C.; *Yhnell* v. *D.P.P.* [1989] R.T.R. 250, D.C.; *Thomas* v. *D.P.P., The Times,* October 17, 1989, D.C.; *Thompson* v. *Allan,* 1989 S.L.T. 868; *Dickinson* v. *D.P.P.* [1989] Crim.L.R. 741, D.C.; *Milne* v. *Westwater,* 1990 S.C.C.R. 46; *McDade* v. *Jessop,* 1990 S.C.C.R. 156; *Oswald* v. *D.P.P.* [1989] R.T.R. 360, D.C.; *Gardner* v. *D.P.P.* [1989] R.T.R. 384, D.C.; *Davies* v. *D.P.P.* [1989] R.T.R. 391, D.C.; *D.P.P.* v. *Gordon; D.P.P.* v. *Griggs* [1990] R.T.R. 71, D.C.; *D.P.P.* v. *Byrne, The Times,* October 10, 1990, C.A.

s. 9, see *Askew* v. *D.P.P.* [1988] R.T.R. 303, D.C.; *Smith* v. *Wilson,* 1989 S.C.C.R. 395.

s. 10, see *Gumbley* v. *Cunningham* [1989] 2 W.L.R. 1, H.L.; *Hassan* v. *Scott,* 1989 S.L.T. 380; *Beauchamp-Thompson* v. *D.P.P.* [1989] R.T.R. 54, D.C.; *D.P.P.* v. *Williams* [1989] Crim.L.R. 382, D.C.; *Millard* v. *D.P.P.., The Daily Telegraph,* February 22, 1990, D.C.; *Garner* v. *D.P.P.* (1990) 90 Cr.App.R. 178; [1989] Crim.L.R. 583, D.C.

ss. 10, 12, see *Oswald* v. *D.P.P.* [1989] R.T.R. 360, D.C.

s. 12, see *D.P.P.* v. *Frost* [1989] R.T.R. 11, D.C.; *Beauchamp-Thompson* v. *D.P.P.* [1989] R.T.R. 54, D.C.; *Thompson* v. *Allan,* 1989 S.L.T. 868.

s. 22, see *O'Halloran* v. *D.P.P.* [1989] 87 L.G.R. 748; [1990] J.P.N. 598, D.C.

s. 25, see *R.* v. *Kingston upon Thames Crown Court, ex p. Scarll, The Times,* April 28, 1989, D.C.; *D.P.P.* v. *Drury* [1989] R.T.R. 165, D.C.; *Martin* v. *Hamilton,* 1989 S.L.T. 860; *Hynd* v. *O'Brien,* 1990 S.C.C.R. 129.

s. 40, see *Travel-Gas (Midlands)* v. *Reynolds; Walton* v. *Reynolds; Myers (J.H.)* v. *Licensing Authority for the North Eastern Traffic Area* [1989] R.T.R. 75, D.C.; *N.F.C. Forwarding* v. *D.P.P.* [1989] R.T.R. 239, D.C.

s. 43, regs. 89/321.

s. 45, regs. 89/320.

s. 50, regs. 89/350.

s. 85, regs. 89/762.

s. 87, see *McFarlane* v. *Secretary of State for Scotland* (Sh.Ct.), 1988 S.C.L.R. 623.

CAP.

1972—cont.

20. Road Traffic Act 1972—cont.

s. 87, regs. 89/373.

s. 93, see *McLeod* v. *MacDougall,* 1989 S.L.T. 151; *D.P.P.* v. *O'Meara* [1989] R.T.R. 24, D.C.; *Beauchamp-Thompson* v. *D.P.P.* [1989] R.T.R. 54, D.C; *D.P.P.* v. *Waller* [1989] R.T.R. 112, D.C.; *R.* v. *Buckley* [1989] Crim.L.R. 386, C.A.; *McDade* v. *Jessop,* 1990 S.C.C.R. 156; *Att.-Gen.'s References (Nos. 3 and 5 of 1989)* [1989] R.T.R. 337, C.A.; *D.P.P.* v. *Barker* [1990] R.T.R. 1, D.C.; *D.P.P.* v. *Younas* [1990] R.T.R. 22, D.C.; *Smith* v. *D.P.P.* [1990] R.T.R. 17, D.C.; *Gardner* v. *D.P.P.* [1989] R.T.R. 384, D.C.

s. 99, see *Cherry* v. *Walkingshaw,* 1989 S.C.C.R. 256.

s. 101, see *Robinson* v. *D.P.P.* [1989] R.T.R. 421, D.C; *D.P.P.* v. *Fruer; Same* v. *Siba; Same* v. *Ward* [1989] R.T.R. 29, D.C.; *McDade* v. *Jessop,* 1990 S.C.C.R. 156.

s. 101, regs. 89/373.

s. 107, regs. 89/762.

s. 112, see *Hall Construction Services* v. *D.P.P.* [1989] R.T.R. 399, D.C.

s. 143, see *McGuinness* v. *Jessop,* 1989 S.C.C.R. 349.

s. 145, see *Limbrick* v. *French and Farley,* Simon Brown J., June 8, 1989.

s. 148, see *Pitts* v. *Hunt* [1989] 3 W.L.R. 795, Fallon Q.C.

s. 149, see *Harrington* v. *Link Motor Policies at Lloyd's* [1989] R.T.R. 345, C.A.

s. 168, see *McMahon* v. *Cardle,* 1988 S.C.C.R. 556; *Hingston* v. *Pollock,* 1989 S.C.C.R. 697.

s. 176, see *Martin* v. *Hamilton,* 1989 S.L.T. 860.

s. 177, see *Att.-Gen.'s References (Nos. 3 and 5 of 1989)* [1989] R.T.R. 337, C.A.

s. 179, see *D.P.P.* v. *Pidhajeckyi, The Times,* November 27, 1990, D.C.

sch. 4, see *R.* v. *Waltham Forest Justices, ex p. Barton, The Times,* April 19, 1989, D.C.; *R.* v. *Rhuddlan Justices, ex p. O'Connor* [1989] Crim.L.R. 374, D.C.; *McDade* v. *Jessop,* 1990 S.C.C.R. 156; *Att.-Gen.'s References (Nos. 3 and 5 of 1989)* [1989] R.T.R. 337, C.A.; *D.P.P.* v. *Younas* [1990] R.T.R. 22, D.C.; *Gardner* v. *D.P.P.* [1989] R.T.R. 384, D.C.

28. Employment Medical Advisory Service Act 1972.

ss. 5, 8, repealed in pt. (prosp.): 1989, c.38, sch.7.

sch. 2, repealed in pt.: regs. 89/682.

35. Defective Premises Act 1972.

s. 4, see *Kay McNerny* v. *Lambeth London Borough Council* (1988) 21 H.L.R. 188, C.A.

41. Finance Act 1972.

ss. 67–69, repealed: 1990, c.1, sch.2.

s. 85, see *Proctor & Gamble* v. *Taylerson (Inspector of Taxes)* [1988] S.T.C. 854, Vinelott J.

ss. 85, 100, see *Collard (Inspector of Taxes)* v. *Mining and Industrial Holdings* [1989] S.T.C. 384, H.L.

s. 86, see *Union Texas Petroleum Corp.* v. *Critchley (Inspector of Taxes)* [1988] S.T.C. 691, Harman J.

schs. 11, 21, regs. 90/1147.

sch. 24, repealed in pt.: 1989, c.26, sch.17; 1990, c.29, sch.19.

41

iii) The Law Reports Index has an index at the back which cites cases which have dealt with statutory law (see Chapters 8 and 9).

H   Using 'Words and Phrases' to Interpret Statutes

'Words and Phrases Legally Defined' (Butterworths), is a useful multi-volume publication which defines the more common words and phrases to be found in statutory law. Most law libraries will keep it.

I   The Use of Hansard to Interpret Statutes

The recent House of Lords decision in *Pepper v Hart* [1992] 3 WLR 1032 allows courts now to refer to Hansard whenever there is an ambiguity in the piece of legislation under consideration. Hansard publishes the speeches of the promoter of the legislation and any debates carried on in the Houses of Parliament. If a speech of the promoter makes the intention of the legislature very clear in relation to the whole of the statute or a particular section, it can be used. Most law libraries keep Hansard.

J   Introduction to Statutory Instruments

1 How to find statutory instruments

Statutory instruments are generally made by the Ministers or departments of the government, under powers given to them by statutes. The rules produced are usually refered to as regulations. It is important not to assume that these regulations are less important than statutes—they acquire statutory status by being made under the 'parent' statute. Statutory instruments (S.I.s) are made in all areas of the law, and cover procedural and substantive aspects.

If you have a citation for a statutory instrument, you need to interpret that citation. For example, 1991 S.I. No. 245 means the 245th statutory instrument of 1991. There are two main ways of then obtaining a copy of it:

i)   Halsbury's Statutory Instruments;

ii) the original government publications.

Halsbury's Statutory Instruments (Butterworths)

These are arranged in volumes by subject matter, just like Halsbury's Laws and Halsbury's Statutes. There is a general index which lists all S.I.s by year and number, and separate index listing them alphabetically by title. The indexes will refer you to the relevant volume. The only problem with Halsbury's is that quite often once you find the right page of the right volume you find a summary of the statutory instrument instead of a complete copy. In that case, you'll need to turn to the second method.

The original government publications (HMSO)

These can generally be found in the library somewhere near Halsbury's Statutory Instruments, in boxes. There will be several boxes for each year and the spine will tell you which S.I.s are to be found inside (for example, 1990 S.I. Nos. 189-936). Inside, the S.I.s will be arranged numerically.

Alternatively, if you know what area of law the S.I. is concerned with, you will generally find a complete copy in the relevant loose-leaf encyclopaedia, or in the various Butterworth's Handbooks to the particular area of law, as referred to earlier.

2   How to read and understand statutory instruments

When reading statutory instruments you should bear in mind the same rules as for statutes. See the six-point plan above.

3   How to find recent statutory instruments

Encyclopaedias covering the area of law you are concerned with all have regular updating bulletins which will usually tell you of the publication of the latest S.I.s, with a brief summary. Current Law's monthly update will also refer you to them under the relevant subject heading. Halsbury's Statutory Instruments also has an updating volume. Unfortunately, in order to find the latest S.I.s in complete form you will have to look at the loose-leaf copies produced by HMSO. If your law library has a computer catalogue, then if you type in your subject area and enter, it will produce the latest statutory instruments. But even computer indexes are often two weeks out of date.

K   Procedural Rules

1   Civil procedure

The High Court

The rules relating to civil procedure in the High Court can be found in the Supreme Court Act 1981 and in the Rules of the Supreme Court 1965, as amended on numerous occasions since. These can easily and most conveniently be found in The Supreme Court Practice (White Book). This can be found in all law libraries and is absolutely essential for all civil practitioners. The first volume contains the Rules of the Supreme Court, arranged in Orders as they are known, and the second, the Supreme Court Act, other relevant statutes and forms. The weekly 'Supreme Court News' will inform you of the latest changes.

When you see 'RSC Ord 53, r 3' this is refering you to a rule of the Supreme Court – here one of the rules relating to judicial review. It can be found in the first volume of the White Book.

The County Court

The rules relating to civil procedure in the County Court are contained in the County Court Act 1984 and the County Court Rules. Each can easily be found in The County Court Practice (Green Book). A new edition is produced each year and there are supplements to inform you of more recent law. When you see 'CCR. Ord 16, r 1' this is referring you to one of the rules of the County Court.

2 Criminal procedure

The most important statute which covers procedure in the Magistrates' Courts is the Magistrates Courts Act 1980. A copy of this, with commentary can obviously be found in Halsbury's Statutes. As for other rules relating to Magistrates Courts, these can most easily be found in 'Stone's Justices Manual' - a three volume publication concerned especially with procedural and substantive law in the Magistrates Courts. These other rules are not set out in a complete body of rules as in the High Court and County Court, but are the product of various different statutory instruments. In particular, bear in mind the Magistrates Courts Rules (1981 S.I. No. 553).

As for the Crown Court, there is no one particular statute which covers the majority of the rules relating to Crown Court procedure. However, statutes to consider are Juries Act 1974; Indictments Act 1915; and, in relation to appeals, the Criminal Appeal Act 1968. Crown Court rules created under various statutory instruments can easily be found in Archbold's Pleading, Evidence and Practice manual, volume 1. This publication is considered to be essential for most Crown Court Criminal practitioners.

Important statutes covering procedural law in both the Magistrates' and the Crown Court are the Bail Act 1976; The Prosecution of Offences Act 1985; Criminal Justice Act 1988 and the Criminal Justice Act 1991.

REVIEW

Questions

1   What is the easiest way to find a copy of a statute?

2   What is the easiest way to find a copy of a statutory instrument?

3   How do you ensure the statute is in force?

4   How do you find very recent legislation?

5   How do you find cases which apply or interpret the statute?

6   What are the basic interpretive resources?

7   What are the six rules for the reading of statutory law?

8   What are statutory instruments?

Answers

1   Halsbury's Statutes (Butterworths); or Current Law Statutes Annotated.

2   Halsbury's Statutory Instruments (Butterworths).

3   Check Halsbury's, 'Is It In Force?'

4   Check 'Archbold News' or 'The Supreme Court News', produced weekly, or Current Law's monthly editions to see what legislation has been passed very recently, and then Halsbury's Statutes latest Supplement if you want a copy. Check your computer catalogue under a relevant subject heading if your library has one.

5   Check Current Law Legislation Citator (Sweet & Maxwell), which will list cases, with their citations, which refer to and/or interpret the statute or statutory instrument you are concerned with. See also the Law Reports Index.

6   Bennion on 'Statutory Interpretation'; the interpretation

or definitions section in the legislation itself;
Interpretation Act 1978; any legal dictionary; and
Hansard.

7   Read the statute at least three times; pay close attention to
'ands' and 'ors'; assume all words and punctuation in the
statute have meaning; interpret a statute so that it is
consistent with other related statutes; interpret the
statute so that it makes sense or does not lead to
improbable results; track down all cross-references to
other statutes or sections.

8   Statutory instruments are regulations created under a
statute by government ministers or departments.

Chapter 7

Understanding Case Law

Finding the right court decision (case) is the heart of the legal research method outlined in Chapter 2. No matter how clear a statute or regulation may seem on its face—and few fit that description—you need to find out what the courts have done with it in situations like yours. And the best path to that result is first to find one relevant case that, through the cross-reference materials covered in Chapter 9, will lead you to others.

This chapter introduces you to cases—what they are and how they influence later disputes.

A   How Cases are Organised

It is the published judgments of the higher courts that make up most of the cases that you will find reported. You will find a list of the most important law reports in Chapter 5.

1   How the case report and judgment are organised

Normally every case report contains five elements - the 'headnotes'; the names of solicitors and barristers involved; a list of caselaw and statutory law referred to in case; the arguments of counsel followed by the judgment. The judgment contains a statement of facts; a statement of the legal issues involved; the decision made or order given; and the reasons for so deciding or ordering.

A detailed statement of the facts will usually be given by the court, the facts being the ones the court has determined to be the true or which the court below has determined to be true.

When stating its decision, the court will give a ruling or holding. If the court is a court of appeal, then it will 'affirm' the decision of the court below or 'uphold' it if it agrees with the decision given below. If the court disagrees with the court below it will 'overturn', 'overrule' or 'reverse' the lower court's decision.

Sometimes the higher court will order a retrial in the court below. This occurs most often when the High Court judicially reviews the decision made in a magistrates court, or where the Criminal Court of Appeal quashes a conviction on the grounds of procedural errors.

By far the most important part of a judgment is the reasoning. This is usually the longest part of the case and the most difficult to understand. The reasoning of judges will become complicated if the legal issues are complicated or if the law is undecided. The most important part of legal training, especially at the Bar, is learning how to analyse this element of case reports, but with a little effort any legal researcher should get the hang of the basics. This chapter should help.

Below (pages 107–110) is a copy of a short case report. In this particular case the headnotes are followed by the list of lawyers and the list of law referred to and then the judgment, including a statement of facts, a statement of the legal issues involved, the reasoning and the order made. Not all case reports will follow this pattern, but most place the elements of the case report in this order.

2   Using headnotes to understand a case

Headnotes are to be found at the beginning of a case and generally consist of a short summary of the facts, what the parties were trying to obtain, the legal issues involved and then a number of paragraphs (the number depends on the complexity of the case) giving the ruling and a brief summary of the reasons for so doing. The headnotes will usually also mention the previous caselaw followed, overturned or distinguished. The caselaw merely considered is generally not mentioned in the headnotes but before the judgment a list of all cases mentioned in argument or in the judgment can be found.

The paragraphs in the headnotes will be in the sequence that the particular issues are to be found in the judgment and usually give a reference. That is, at the end of the paragraph there will be one or more pages mentioned in brackets, eg 124B–125A, meaning that this particular legal issue is discussed in the judgment between these pages and paragraphs. Almost all law reports letter their pages A–H. This can be very useful because if you only wish to find the discussion in the judgment on one legal issue out of six, then you need not trawl through the whole judgment.

624 [1992] 1 FLR

MIR v MIR

A

Family Division

Scott Baker J

16 October 1991

B

Contempt of court – Sequestration – Father removing ward outside jurisdiction without court's consent – Writ of sequestration against father's assets within jurisdiction to finance mother's litigation for return of ward by letting or as security for loan – Mother applying for leave for sequestrators to sell property – Whether court having power to order sequestrated property to be sold

The father of the ward was in contempt of court for removing the ward to Pakistan C and failing to return him. On 13 June 1991 the President made an order committing the father to prison for 6 months, suspended on his compliance with the court's order to return the ward within one month. He also granted a writ of sequestration so that sequestrators, acting on the court's instructions, might take possession of the former matrimonial home with leave to let it or to use it as security for a loan, in order that the mother might finance litigation in Pakistan to obtain the ward's return. On the father continuing in contempt of court, the D plaintiff mother sought a variation of the order to enable the sequestrators to sell the property. The Official Solicitor supported the application.

Held – the principle established by *Shaw v Wright* (1796) 3 Ves 22 and *Sutton v Stone* (1745) 1 Dick 107 and treated as good law in 17 Halsbury's Laws of England (4th edn), to the effect that the issue of a writ of sequestration did not empower the court to order the sale of freehold property because there was no procedure whereby good title could be given to the purchaser, no longer applied, by virtue of s 39 of the Supreme Court Act 1981, which provided that where a court had E directed a person to execute any conveyance or other document and that person failed to comply or could not be found, the High Court might order that the conveyance or document be executed. Accordingly, if the husband in the case was ordered by the court to transfer his interest in the matrimonial home to the sequestrators and failed to do so, the court could invoke s 39 in order to achieve the desired result. It followed that the order sought could properly be made in law. Furthermore, it was appropriate, on the facts, in view of the need for the court to F secure compliance with its orders, particularly in the case of wards of court who were being wrongly retained outside the jurisdiction. An order would be made for the father to transfer his interest in the matrimonial home to the sequestrators, and the application for leave to be given to the sequestrators to sell the property would be granted.

Statutory provision considered
Supreme Court Act 1981, s 39

G

Cases referred to in judgment
Ellard v Warren (1681) 3 Rep Ch 87, 21 ER 737
Hipkin v Hipkin [1962] 1 WLR 491, [1962] 2 All ER 155
Richardson v Richardson [1989] Fam 95, [1990] 1 FLR 186, [1989] 3 WLR 865, [1989] 3 All ER 779, FD
Shaw v Wright (1796) 3 Ves 22, 30 ER 872
Sutton v Stone (1745) 1 Dick 107, 21 ER 209

H

Peter Horrocks for the mother
Andrew Tidbury for the Official Solicitor

Short Case Report

[1992] 1 FLR   **Mir v Mir**   **(FD)**   **625**

A   **SCOTT BAKER J**: This is an application for leave to be given to sequestrators to sell 34A Geere Road, Stratford in East London, so that part of the proceeds of sale can be used to finance the cost of proceedings in Pakistan, to secure the return of a ward of court.

The father of the ward is in continuing contempt of court, and should have returned the ward long ago. This case was before the President on 13 June 1991. He made an order committing the father to prison for B   6 months, suspended on his compliance with the court's order within one month, ie to return the ward. I have read a transcript of his judgment. He said:

C   '! shall grant the application for a writ of sequestration so that sequestrators acting on the court's instructions may take possession of the former matrimonial home, with leave to let it or to use it as security for a loan, in order that the mother may finance litigation in Pakistan, directed to seeking the return of . . . (the ward) to this jurisdiction.'

In making that order, the President followed *Richardson v Richardson* [1989] Fam 95, [1990] 1 FLR 186, in which I had made a similar order in respect of a mother's property, she having removed two wards to the D   Republic of Ireland, being there in contempt of court. In *Richardson v Richardson*, the wards were returned, following the order that I made. In this case, the ward has not yet been returned.

Mr Horrocks, who appears on behalf of the plaintiff mother, seeks a variation of the present order, in that he wishes the property, which is the former matrimonial home, to be sold. Mr Tidbury, who acts for the E   Official Solicitor, supports this application.

In *Richardson v Richardson*, Mr Horrocks, who acted for the plaintiff on that occasion too, did not pursue his application for leave for the property to be sold. Consequently, in that case, I did not have to decide whether there was power to make such an order. That point had been left open by Sir Joscelyn Simon P in *Hipkin v Hipkin* [1962] 1 WLR 491 at p 493, where he said:

F

'On further investigation it appears that there are authorities treated as good law in 16 Halsbury's Laws of England (3rd edn), p 76, to the effect that the issue of a writ of sequestration does not empower the court to order the sale of freehold property. Mr Gray told me that Mr Mowbrey was prepared to argue that those authorities are no longer G   binding, but I saw no way of hearing two counsel on a motion such as this and, on the view that I have taken, I did not find it necessary to call for argument on the point. I proceed on the basis that those authorities are effective.'

So the then President left the point open in *Hipkin v Hipkin*, and it was again left open in *Richardson v Richardson*. The point now, however, falls H   to be decided. *17 Halsbury's Laws of England* (4th edn), para 515 says this:

'No property sequestrated can be sold without leave of the court, and no land, except possibly leaseholds, can be ordered to be sold.'

Short Case Report

Then there is a note, note 10, which refers to *Shaw v Wright* (1796) 3   **A**
Ves 22 and *Sutton v Stone* (1745) 1 Dick 107, and also *Hipkin v Hipkin*.
   So Halsbury categorically states that the court does not have the power
to order sale, and refers to these two ancient authorities. Mr Horrocks has
helpfully put these two authorities before the court, and it appears that
there is no other learning on the subject, except, possibly, *Ellard v Warren*
(1681) 3 Rep Ch 87, where sequestrators were ordered to sell a term of   **B**
years to satisfy money due.
   It is of some importance to look and see what was said in *Shaw v Wright*
and *Sutton v Stone*. In *Shaw v Wright*, the Lord Chancellor, Lord
Loughborough, said:

> 'The order (that is an order for sale) would do you no good. I should not   **C**
> have much difficulty in selling, not only perishable commodities, but if
> the sequestrators were in possession of rents paid in kind, or the natural
> produce of a farm; but how shall I make a title? By whom? I cannot well
> order the sequestrators to sell without at the same time warranting the
> title: then I do not know how I can do that. It does not transfer the term
> to the sequestrators. It is only a process to compel an appearance, the
> performance of a duty. All profits I will direct them to apply. The   **D**
> difficulty is this: if the sequestrators sell, and the purchasers should be
> brought before this court to complete their contracts, I could not
> compel them to pay the money. I cannot make a man take a title, which
> he is to support a bill for an injunction. You will not find any instance of
> an order to sell under a sequestration a subject, which passes by title and
> not by delivery.'

Then *Sutton v Stone*, the report of which is very short: **E**

> 'Sequestrators ordered to sell a leasehold estate, sequestered for a duty.
> On a similar application, Lord Loughborough LC refused it, saying
> "Who is to make out the title?"'

So it appears that the underlying reason why the courts in earlier times   **F**
would not make an order for sale of freehold property was the absence of
any procedure whereby good title could be given to the purchaser. It has
been pointed out to me that that difficulty no longer exists today. It is not
uncommon in this Division that, on an ancillary relief application, one
spouse fails to comply with an order to the court to transfer property to the
other spouse. The remedy for this is to be found in s 39 of the Supreme
Court Act 1981, which provides as follows: **G**

> '(1) Where the court has given or made a judgment or order directing
> a person to execute any conveyance, contract or other document, or to
> endorse any negotiable instrument, then if that person –
>   (a) neglects or refuses to comply with the judgment or order, or
>   (b) cannot after reasonable inquiry be found,   **H**
> the High Court may, on such terms and conditions if any as may be just,
> order that the conveyance, contract or other document shall be
> executed, or that the negotiable instrument shall be endorsed by such
> person as the court may nominate for that purpose.

Short Case Report

[1992] 1 FLR   Scott Baker J   Mir v Mir   (FD)   627

A   (2) A conveyance, contract, document or instrument executed or
endorsed in pursuance of an order under this section shall operate and
be for all purposes available as if it had been executed or endorsed by
the person originally directed to execute or endorse it.'

So it is pointed out by Mr Horrocks, and by Mr Tidbury for the Official
Solicitor, that, if I order the husband in this case to transfer his interest in
B   34A Geere Road to the sequestrators, and he fails to do so, I can invoke
s 39 of the Supreme Court Act 1981 in order to achieve the desired result.
Section 39 of the Supreme Court Act emanated from, I think, the
Judicature Act 1925, which in turn emanated from the Judicature Act
1884. But prior to 1884, counsel tell me that there was no such power.
Therefore, it seems that the reason underlying the decisions in *Shaw v
C   Wright* and *Sutton v Stone* really no longer applies.
In the case of *Richardson v Richardson* [1989] Fam 95 at p 102B, [1990]
1 FLR at p 192, I mentioned that, if the property is used as security for a
loan (permitted by the President's order in this case), the time might come
when the security had to be realised by sale of the property. It would be
odd if the law permitted that, but not a direct order for sale.
I have come to the conclusion that the court does everything that it can
D   to secure compliance with its orders, particularly in the case of wards of
court, where they are wrongly being detained out of the jurisdiction. It
seems to me that the order that is sought in this case is an appropriate one,
and is one that I can properly make in law. I therefore grant the relief that
is sought.

Order accordingly.
E
Solicitors: *Young & Lee* for the mother
            Official Solicitor

PATRICIA HARGROVE
Barrister

Short Case Report

N.B. Headnotes can be very useful if you are in a hurry or if the judgment itself makes no sense to you, but it is very important to remember that the judges themselves do not produce them. Headnotes are the creation of the reporter and reporters and editors are fallible. Mistakes can be made. Of course headnotes can usually tell you at a quick glance whether or not a case is relevant, but you must check the judgment itself to be sure. Advocates are allowed to read out headnotes in court, but usually only so long as they read out the relevant part of the judgment as well.

See pages 112-113 for an example of a long headnote.

B   How Precedent Works

Past decisions in appellate and High Court cases are powerful predictors of what the courts are likely to do in future cases given a similar set of facts. Most judges try hard to be consistent with decisions that either they or a higher court have made. This consistency is very important to a just legal system and is the essence of the common law tradition. (Common law—the decisions of courts over the years—is discussed in Chapter 3, An Overview of the Law.) For this reason, if you can find a previous court decision that rules your way on facts similar to your situation, you have a good chance of persuading a judge to follow that case and decide in your favour.

There are two basic principles to understand when you are reading cases with an eye to using them to persuade a judge to rule your way. One is called 'precedent', the other 'persuasive authority'.

1   Precedent

In the legal sense, a 'precedent' is an earlier case that is relevant to a case to be decided. If there is nothing to distinguish the circumstances of the current case from the already-decided one, the earlier holding is considered binding on the court.

The idea of a precedent comes from a basic principle of the English common law system: *stare decisis* (Latin for 'let the decision stand'). Once a high court decides how the law should be applied to a

[1993] IRLR 104

GEC Ferranti Defence Systems v MSF: Lord Coulsfield

ment of the consultation period. There is no attempt to explain why the information provided on 13 September was inadequate, nor any attempt to consider the information provided on 23 September, 26 September, 1 October, or 7 October. The significance of that failure is heightened by the fact that there is nothing pointed to by the Industrial Tribunal to justify its decision to take the date of 24 October 1991 as the commencement date; nor, so far as we can see, are there any facts and circumstances which could provide a ground for holding that date to be the appropriate date. In our opinion, therefore, the decision of the Industrial Tribunal cannot stand. On the other hand, we do not think that there is sufficient material in the documents before us, without some explanation of their significance in relation to the need for effective consultation, to enable us to decide at what point during the process sufficient information was available. In these circumstances, we have no alternative but to allow the appeal and remit the case to a different Industrial Tribunal for rehearing.

R v.
BRITISH COAL CORPORATION and
SECRETARY OF STATE FOR TRADE AND
INDUSTRY ex parte VARDY and others

1000	*European Community law*	
1600	*Handling redundancies*	
1620	*Timing of consultation*	
1640	*Consultation requirements*	
1698	*Effect of European Community law*	
10000	*Judicial review*	

Trade Union and Labour Relations (Consolidation) Act 1992 sections: 179(1), 188(1), 188(2)(a), 188(8), 189
EEC Collective Redundancies Directive 75/129: Articles 1(2), 2(1), 2(2)
Coal Industry Nationalisation Act 1946 sections: 3(1), 46
Coal Industry Act 1987 (as amended) section: 3

The facts:
On 13 October 1992, British Coal announced that it was to close 31 collieries. The announcement said that a "substantial proportion" would be closed "within a few weeks, with production ceasing immediately." It was stated that the employees concerned would receive redundancy payments in excess of the statutory maximum.

On 19 October, however, following protests, the Secretary of State, now known as the President of the Board of Trade, announced that the Government had concluded that British Coal should be allowed to proceed with the closure of only 10 pits which it had identified as loss-making and having no prospect of future viability. He added that "no closure will . . . take place until after the statutory consultation period has been completed." He said that there would be a moratorium on the closure of the remaining 21 pits until after widespread consultation had taken place.

On 30 October, when the consultation process was initiated, the employers stated that they would comply both with the requirements of s.99 of the Employment Protection Act 1975 (now s.198 of the Trade Union and Labour Relations (Consolidation) Act 1992) and EEC Collective Redundancies Directive 75/129.

Mr Vardy and other members of the Union of Democratic Mineworkers brought judicial review proceedings against British Coal challenging as unlawful the decision to close 10 pits without resort to the Modified Colliery Review Procedure (MCRP) or a procedure substantially to the same effect. Proceedings were also brought against the President challenging his decision to authorise or direct British Coal to proceed with the closure of the 10 pits without resort to the MCRP or a procedure substantially to the same effect. The third application was brought by members of the National Union of Mineworkers against both British Coal and the President challenging the decisions of British Coal to close the 10 pits and to cease production at them, thus prejudicing the consultation process; and also challenging the decisions of the President not to instruct British Coal to consult with the unions, not to include the 10 pits in the general review which covered the other 21 pits, and not to instruct British Coal not to cease production pending consultation.

The MCRP sets out a consultation process for the closure of collieries. It was an agreement made in accordance with the obligations placed on the employers by s.46(1) of the Coal Industry Nationalisation Act for the "establishment and maintenance of joint machinery for . . . consultation." It was also intended to comply with the redundancy consultation requirements of the Employment Protection Act and, as modified in 1985, permitted the unions to appeal to an independent review board. The procedure stipulated that the employers would give full weight to the findings of such a board before announcing a final decision on a proposed closure. However, in announcing its decision to close the 31 pits, British Coal took the view that the MCRP could not be operated and that it had not been designed to deal with a "sudden collapse" in the market for coal, such as that which had led to the closure decision.

The High Court, Queen's Bench Division – Divisional Court (Lord Justice Glidewell, Mr Justice Hidden) on 21 December 1992 quashed the decisions announced on 19 October by both the President of the Board of Trade and British Coal and granted a declaration that British Coal should not

Example of long Headnote

reach a final decision on the closure of any of the 10 collieries, nor should the President make available funds which would enable British Coal to reach such a decision, until a procedure substantially to the same effect as the Modified Colliery Review Procedure, including some form of independent scrutiny, had been followed in relation to each of the collieries.

The Divisional Court held:

🖝) 10000 The decisions by both British Coal and the President of the Board of Trade that 31 pits should be closed without any consultation with the trade unions, and their subsequent decisions to close 10 of the 31 collieries and review the future of the remaining 21, were unlawful.

The decisions announced on 13 October 1992 that 31 pits should be closed without any consultation were in breach of the redundancy consultation provisions laid down by s.188 of the Trade Union and Labour Relations (Consolidation) Act 1992 and of EEC Redundancy Consultation Directive 75/129 (if it applied), and wholly disregarded the agreement for the use of the Modified Colliery Review Procedure.

The decisions announced on 19 October, that 10 of the collieries would be closed, again took no account of the agreement to use the MCRP. Like the decisions of 13 October, they were unlawful because they ignored British Coal's obligation under s.46(1) of the Coal Industry Nationalisation Act and completely failed to satisfy the legitimate expectation of the unions and their members that, when British Coal proposed to close any pit or pits, they would consult the relevant unions by using the MCRP, including an independent review board if the unions so wished, and would not withdraw the use of that consultative mechanism without first informing the unions of their intention to do so and giving them a proper opportunity to comment and object. Moreover, if British Coal wished to take this step, s.46(1) obliged them to initiate consultations about an alternative procedure.

In addition, the decision to deprive the unions and workforce at the 10 pits of any independent scrutiny of whether at each of them British Coal's criteria for closing them were met could properly be described as irrational, in that it was one which neither the President nor the employers, having regard to the issues, including the employers' legal obligations, could properly have reached.

All the decisions challenged were matters of public law and susceptible to judicial review. In deciding to make available to British Coal sufficient funds to enable them to make enhanced redundancy payments to miners dismissed as a result of the closures, the President was acting in the exercise of statutory powers under the Coal Industry Act. He was acting under the same statutory powers in deciding to withdraw his earlier decision and for the time being to fund redundancy payments only for the employees at 10 pits, subject to statutory consultation. The decisions by

British Coal were public law decisions rather than commercial decisions within the area of private law because the Coal Industry Nationalisation Act 1946 imposes on British Coal a particular obligation as to consultation in respect of colliery closures and resulting redundancies which is wider than that imposed by s.188 of the 1992 Act and the Directive, and which applies only to the coalmining industry. It places express duties upon British Coal which are not placed on other major employers in private ownership.

The decisions announced on 19 October were ineffective in law and would be quashed. There was no need to give relief with regard to the unlawful decisions of 13 October, since they were rendered ineffective by the decisions of 19 October. The appropriate relief was a declaration which would add some independent scrutiny to the consultations which had already started in accordance with both s.188 and Directive 75/129. It was because that was lacking that British Coal were failing not merely to follow the MCRP but to put in its place any procedure substantially to the same effect.

Obiter dicta (per Glidewell LJ):

1620 Section 188 of the Trade Union and Labour
1640 Relations (Consolidation) Act does not re-
1698 quire a consultation about the reasons for a redundancy, including whether or not a plant should close. The Court agreed with the statement in *Harvey on Industrial Relations and Employment Law* that the obligation is not so much to consult with the unions on whether there should be redundancies, but rather to consult on how to carry out any redundancy programme which management deems necessary. In any event, the right to a protective award under s.189 is a private law right, and breach of the statutory obligation would not be susceptible to judicial review.

In contrast, the fact that EEC Directive 75/129 provides that consultations are to begin as soon as the employer contemplates redundancies and that they are to include ways and means of avoiding redundancies indicates that the Directive is to be interpreted as including consultation on ways of avoiding redundancies by not closing the particular establishment, if that is what the employer has in mind.

Moreover, the Directive envisages consultation at an early stage when the employer is first envisaging the possibility that he may have to make employees redundant. Section 188 applies when he has decided that it is his intention, however reluctant, to make employees redundant.

The difference between the wording of the Directive and the wording of s.188 is such that the section cannot be interpreted as having the same meaning as the Directive.

Cases referred to:
R v Panel on Takeovers and Mergers ex parte Datafin plc [1987] 1 QB 815 CA

Example of long Headnote

Here '1620', '1640' and '1698' refer to the relevant paragraphs in the judgment which deal with these issues.

particular set of facts, this decision controls later decisions by that and lower courts. The one exception to this is the House of Lords which is not bound to follow its earlier decisions.

A case is only a precedent as to its particular decision, ie its *ratio decidendi*, and the law necessary to arrive at that decision. If, in passing, a judge deals with a legal question that is not absolutely essential to the decision, the reasoning and opinion in respect to this tangential question are not precedent, but non-binding *obiter dicta*.

It is common for courts to avoid overruling earlier decisions by distinguishing the earlier one from the present one on the basis of some insignificant factual difference or small legal issue. It is much easier to get a court to 'distinguish' an old case than openly overrule it. Simply put, it is sometimes difficult to tell whether an earlier case has been overruled (and is clearly no longer precedent) or distinguished (and therefore technically still operative as precedent). (See Chapter 11, *The Legal Research Method: Examples*.) However, the headnotes will often make it clear if a case is followed, distinguished or overruled.

A case is only precedent as to a particular set of facts and the precise legal issue decided in light of those facts. The more the facts or legal issues vary between two cases, the less the former operates as precedent in respect to the latter. Learning the art of distinguishing cases on the basis of the facts and issues decided takes some time.

Precedent is essentially determined by the effect later cases have had on the particular case you are considering. The *ratio decidendi* of a case is the central principle upon which the case is decided by the judge or judges. This ratio is not always easy to determine. The headnotes will give you a clue as to where to start. Generally, the ratio is the answer or answers to the question or questions asked by one of both of the parties. Any law interpreted by the court in order to determine that answer is also part of the precedent. Anything else is *obiter*.

How later courts use the case will determine how its ratio changes. For example, a later court may apply the original ratio to a wider set of facts, and so open the ratio up. For example, the court in the first case finds that if a local education authority neglects to suspend one of its teachers who has assaulted a child in the teacher's school, it will be liable to another member of the public who suffers at the hands of that teacher a month later. A later case may apply this principle as precedent to a case involving a local authority which neglects to dismiss a social worker who assaults a foster-parent. The ratio of the original case has been widened so that whenever a local authority employee or local education authority teacher assaults any person they meet in a professional capacity and the local authorities ignore the act and refuse to take action, the local authority will be liable. The ratio may be widened further in a future case to cover all public body employees who assault or otherwise harm members of the public. This is how the law expands.

2 Persuasive authority

If a case is not precedent, and therefore not binding on the court considering it, but contains an excellent analysis of the legal issues involved, it can provide guidance to the court. This is known as 'persuasive authority'. For example the Court of Appeal may consider a judgment of the High Court persuasive if it contains a thorough analysis of the caselaw and/or statutory law. Judgments given in Commonwealth courts can be persuasive as although they are not binding they often concern law which is the same as English law. Decisions of the Privy Council are not binding but are highly persuasive. The Privy Council is the final court of appeal for some Commonwealth countries such as Hong Kong. It is a court made up of the judges of our House of Lords, and so their views are thought to be well worth considering. As a general rule, the higher the court the more persuasive its opinion.

3 How to analyse the effect of an earlier case on your issue

Reading cases and understanding how they apply to your issue can be vexing. You may have to put in a number of hours of practice before you feel comfortable with the case analysis process.

Steps to analysing the effect of an earlier case

Step 1 Identify the precise issues decided in the case—that is, what issues of law the court had to decide in order to make its ruling.

Step 2 Compare the issues in the case to the issues you are interested in and decide whether the case addresses one or more of them. If so, move to Step 3. If not, the case is probably not helpful.

Step 3 Carefully read and understand the facts underlying the case and compare them to the facts of your situation. Does the case's decision on the relevant issues logically stand up when applied to your facts? If so move to Step 4. If not, go to Step 5.

Step 4 Determine whether the court that decided the case you are reading creates precedent for the trial or appellate court you may be dealing with. If so, the case may serve as precedent. If not, move to Step 5.

Step 5 Carefully read and understand the legal reasoning employed by the court when deciding the relevant issues and decide whether it logically would help another court resolve your issues? If so, the case may be persuasive authority.

Around the law

You can often find two lawyers in the same courtroom relying on the same case to support two diametrically opposed positions. This is, at least in part, because lawyers are adept at hairsplitting. Distinguishing one very similar factual situation from another so that the distinguished case will not be used as precedent or persuasive authority in the case you are arguing is a highly developed art.

REVIEW

Questions

1 What is a 'case' for the purpose of discussing the law?

2 What elements does every judgment contain?

3 What is a dissenting opinion and what effect does it have?

4 What is a concurring opinion and what effect does it have?

5 How are headnotes helpful in legal research?

6 What is a precedent?

7 What is persuasive authority?

Answers

1 Cases are the published judgments of appellate and other courts.

2 Almost all published cases contain:

   • a detailed statement of the facts that are accepted by the court as true;

   • a statement of the legal issue or issues presented by the parties for resolution;

   • an answer to the issues presented for resolution—this is called the ruling or holding;

   • a discussion of why the ruling was made—the court's reasoning or rationale.

3 A justice in an appellate court who disagrees with the decision of the majority on a case may issue a dissenting opinion, which is published along with the majority's opinion. No matter how passionate a dissent happens to be, it has no effect on the particular case. However, it may have a persuasive effect on judges in future court decisions.

4   A justice who agrees with the majority decision but disagrees with the reasons given for it may issue a concurring opinion, which is published along with the majority's opinion. A concurring opinion can also have a persuasive influence on future court decisions.

5   They serve as a table of contents to the opinion and they are very helpful when you wish to determine the issues in the case very quickly.

6   An earlier case that is relevant to a case to be decided. If there is nothing to distinguish the circumstances of the current case from the already-decided one, the earlier holding is considered binding on any lower court or court of the same level. This does not apply to the House of Lords. A case is only precedent as to a particular set of facts and the precise legal issue decided in light of those facts.

7   If a case is not precedent, binding on later courts, but contains an excellent analysis of the legal issues and provides guidance for any court which happens to read it, it is 'persuasive authority'.

Chapter 8

Finding Cases

Every reported case has a unique citation. As long as you have the citation and the relevant law reporter in the library, you can find any case. This chapter tells you how to interpret these citations and how to find cases.

A   Interpreting Case Citations

A case citation consists of five items:

(i) the names of the parties involved;

(ii) the year the case is reported;

(iii) the number of the volume of the law reporter in which the case report is to be found;

(iv) the law reporter which holds the case;

(v) the page in the law reporter.

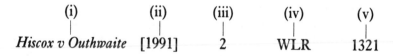

(i)	(ii)	(iii)	(iv)	(v)
Hiscox v Outhwaite	[1991]	2	WLR	1321

This law reporter is the Weekly Law Reports. The case is to be found in volume two at page 1321.

Most citations are in this form. There may be slight variations, for example, there may only be one volume for a particular year, and so the citation will just read [1964] AC 23, for the Appeal Cases law reporter. Also, the law reports of the daily newspapers will have the following citations, by way of example, *R v North West Thames RHA, ex p Daniels* (1993) *The Times*, 22 June; *R v Chief Constable of Avon and Somerset, ex p Clarke* (1986) *Independent*, 28 November.

Most reporters will have the square brackets around the year, thus [1993]; others will have the round brackets, thus (1993). The daily newspaper reports all have round brackets, as well as the Criminal Appeal Reports (Cr App Rep); the older law reporters, eg Coxs' Criminal Cases (Cox CC), or the Queens Bench Division reports (QBD); The Times Law Reports (TLR); the Local Government Reports (LGR); and the law reports contained in journals, eg the Solicitors' Journal (Sol J), and the Estates Gazette (EG). All the major law reporters use the square brackets, eg Appeal Cases (AC); Queens Bench Division Reports (QB); Weekly Law Reports (WLR); All England Law Reports (All. E.R.); Chancery Division Reports (Ch D) and Lloyd's Law Reports (Lloyd's Law Rep).

1 The case name

There are two or more parties involved in a case, and the case name usually includes the first party on each side. The parties may be companies, firms, individuals, societies, or government authorities. In criminal cases, unless it is a private prosecution, the case name will always be *R v Smith*, the *R* standing for *Regina*, ie the Crown, who is prosecuting. Smith is the surname of the defendant, or the first defendant. In civil law, the case only involves the Crown when it concerns judicial review. When you see a name like *R v Essex County Council, ex p Stewart*, this is a judicial review case. The Crown is, effectively considering a review of the decision of Essex County Council, a public body; and Stewart, the individual who wishes to see the Council's decision against him reviewed is an interested party. Nevertheless, Stewart will make the application, and hence will be the Applicant, and Essex County Council will be the Respondent.

The '*v*' stands for 'versus' and is referred to as 'and' when the case name is spoken. In civil cases the first name is the name of the applicant or plaintiff, and the second name, after '*v*' is the name of the respondent or the defendant. Even when the defendant or respondent loses at first instance and seeks to appeal, the case name remains the same despite the fact that the defendant or respondent is now the appellant. In criminal cases it is the same.

There are some exceptions to the general rules. For example, in cases involving juveniles when the court will not allow the name of the child to be disclosed, the case name will be *In re M*, or *In re A*, which mean '*In the matter of M*' or '*In the matter of A*'. Sometimes you will see *C v C*, which usually means it is a family case but the parents' names are not disclosed to protect the interests of the child involved. In criminal cases you will sometimes see *R v M*, which either means a juvenile is being prosecuted, or an adult and the case involves a child victim who could be identified if the adult is.

2 The year in the citation

Every citation has a year. This is the year the case is reported in the particular law reporter, which will not necessarily be the same year the case was decided by the court. On a number of occasions you will come across the same case being reported in 1989 in the Weekly Law Reports and in a different year in the All England Law Reports. It depends on who is quickest to get the case published.

3 The volume number

Sometimes law reporters are numbered consecutively each year. For example, the Criminal Appeal Reports started with volume number 1 when first published. So you will see a citation such as (1989) 91 Cr App Rep 132. This means the case was reported in this reporter in 1989 in the 91st volume of the Criminal Appeal Reports ever produced. The particular case can be found at page 132. Alternatively, you will see volumes numbered within particular years. For example, if in 1994 there are a large number of cases for the All England Law Reports reporter to publish, then there will be more than one volume. Therefore you may see the citation [1994] 3 All ER 567. This means the case you want will be found at page 567 of the third volume of that reporter for 1994. Most of the major law reporters use the latter system for numbering their volumes.

4 The name of the law reporter

Some of the major law reporters have been mentioned above, with their abbreviations. For a more exhaustive list, see Chapter 5. Most of their names make it clear what sort of cases they report. For example, the Queens Bench Reports (QB) will cover cases involving contract law, torts, sale of goods and judicial review among other things. The Chancery Division Reports (Ch D) will cover probate, bankruptcy, trusts and land law. The Weekly Law Reports and the All England Law Reports cover all topics, including the more important criminal cases. The Lloyd's Law Reports (Lloyd's Law Rep) cover commercial law, especially shipping and insurance.

Do not worry about memorising the abbreviations for the law reports straight away — they will come to you naturally after a while. At first you can always check the list of law reporters which all law libraries should have in the office or at the entrance. These should give the abbreviations in alphabetical order and give the law reporter's full name.

5 The page number

This will come last in any citation. If there has been a typing error just check the index at the front of the volume. It is advisable to take down the whole of a citation when you are doing your legal research because mistakes are made. If you do not have the case name and discover the page you have been referred to is obviously not the correct one you will be unable to check the index for the correct page. This will result in frustration if the volume contains forty to fifty law reports.

6 Parallel citations

Case reports are often found in more than one law reporter and so you may want to look at another law reporter's version. A great many people believe that some law reporters are better than others. For example, if your case could be in the QB, Ch D, or AC reporters then ideally you should use that version as it will have been approved by the judge(s) involved. The Weekly Law Reports are considered better than the All England Law Reports by some. So if you have a citation for one reporter its always an idea to check if the case has been reported in a better publication

How do you find a parallel citation?

The easiest way is to refer to the background resource which gave you the case name. Most textbooks, encyclopaedias and digests will give you all the reporters where the case can be found. In addition, or alternatively, refer to the Law Reports Index. This publication has already been mentioned on a number of occasions in this book and it is a publication you should remember and get to know. It is the bible of the legal researcher. In the front is an alphabetical list of all cases reported in the main law reporters for the years covered by that LRI volume. Each of the LRI volumes cover ten years, with paperback editions covering the most recent case reports – usually produced every three months. The volumes are red hardbacks and the paperbacks are pink. The LRI can usually be found on a shelf somewhere near the main law reporters, ie the Weekly Law Reports; the All England Law Reports; and the Appeal Cases, Queens Bench and Chancery Division Reports.

If your case name is *Sweet v Arnold Holdings plc* [1987] but you only have one citation, look at the case in the list at the front of the LRI volume for 1981-1990. This will give you the name of every reporter that your case has been reported in, with a full citation.

B   How to Find Cases

There are a number of ways to do this depending on where you are heading in your research.

- If you have found a relevant statute and want to read cases that interpret the provisions you are interested in, you can probably find an appropriate citation in the case notes following the statute (subsection 2 below) or in the listings for that statute in Current Law Legislation Citator or Law Reports Index (subsection 3 below).

- If your research involves primarily common law (cases), you might find a helpful citation in a background resource (subsection 1 below) or in the subject index to a digest (subsection 4 below), or the Law Reports Index (the 'Index') or the Current Law Case Citator.

- If you know the name of a case that you want to find but not its citation, you can use the Table of Cases in a digest or Index (subsection 5 below). If the case is very recent (within the past several months) and not yet listed in the Index or digest Table of Cases, you can find it by searching the recently published case reporter volumes (subsection 6 below), or the Daily Law Reports Index (on computer or on file).

- If you have a case citation for one reporter and you need the citation for a second reporter (that is, the parallel citation), you can find it by using the Index.

Below we examine in more detail each of these approaches to finding an appropriate citation to that one good case.

1 Background resources

Most of the background materials, discussed in Chapter 5, have a large number of footnotes with citations to cases that discuss specific points of law covered in the main discussion.

2 Case notes that follow statutes

If you are searching for a case that has interpreted a relevant statute, check the listings after the text of the statute in an 'annotated' volume, such as Halsbury's or Current Law Statutes Annotated.

Halsbury's has about fifty volumes, arranged alphabetically by subject matter. Use the separate index volume—which lists statutes alphabetically and chronologically—to find the statute you want. Current Law has a larger number of volumes arranged by year. So the Criminal Justice Act 1991 can be found in one of the volumes for 1991. Check the notes under the relevant section and it will point you to relevant caselaw.

3 Other methods for finding cases which interpret legislation

The most useful tool available to the legal researcher to find cases which consider and interpret statutes and statutory instruments is the Current Law Legislation Citator. This is produced in paperback and has a one list for statutes and one for statutory instruments. The lists cite the legislation chronologically and, within a particular year, alphabetically. Within the particular piece of legislation, the lists separate the section, schedule, part or paragraph numbers, and give you any relevant case names with their citations.

Another method for finding case law which covers legislation is by looking at the Current Law Yearbook for the relevant year. These are blue hardbacks. This will have a subject index at the back in any event which may be of use to you, with reference to brief summaries of cases. But, more importantly there will be a statute citator and a statutory instrument citator at the back. These are organised in the same way as the Current Law Legislation Citator, and will refer you to any relevant cases under a particular section, schedule, etc., with their citations. You can then take a note of the case name and citation and either look at the summary of the case available in the main text of Yearbook, or go straight to the reporter for the full case. Current Law produces monthly editions which are blue paperbacks and are extremely useful for finding more recent cases.

A further method is to use the Law Reports Index, referred to earlier. This has summaries of cases under subject headings, much like the Current Law Yearbook. See the copy of two pages from the Index below (pages 128–129).

The Index also has a list of parts of legislation referred to in cases reported in the years covered by that particular volume of the Index. These can be found at the back. Again the names and citations will be given and you can look at the summaries and find the full report in the best reporter.

Finally, for the most recent case law available you will have to look further than Current Law as even their monthly editions will not cover cases decided in the last few months. The Daily Law Reports Index is available in most law libraries as a publication and on computer. The Daily Law Reports Index can be found in large red hardbacks, with the most recent cases in a binder. Relevant cases can be found by using the index at the back –there is a subject index, and a legislation index which will refer you to cases which

86   Subject Matter

DEFAMATION—*continued*
  Fair comment—*continued*
    Test of fairness
      Plaintiff's article published in newspaper—Newspaper publishing le.ter defamatory of
      plaintiff written in reaction to article—Whether letter comment or statement of fact—
      Whether letter to be read with article or in isolation—Whether on.is on defendant to
      establish belief in views expressed
                 Telnikoff v. Matusevitch, C.A. [1991] 1 Q.B. 102; [1990] 3 W.L.R. 725
                         H.L.(E.) [1992] 2 A.C. 343; [1991] 3 W.L.R. 952

  Parties
    Corporation
      Publication relating to administration of local authority's superannuatio.i fund—Publication
      insinuating maladministration of pension funds—Balance between public interest in
      freedom of speech and protection of authority's reputation—Whether local authority
      entitled to maintain action in respect of governmental and administrative function—Local
      Government Act 1972, s. 222(1)   **Derbyshire County Council v. Times Newspapers Ltd.,**
                               Morland J. [1992] Q.B. 770
                            C.A. [1992] Q.B. 770; [1992] 3 W.L.R. 28

  Pleadings
    Defamatory meaning
      Whether words complained of capable of bearing defamatory meaning—-Whether triable as
      preliminary issue—R.S.C., Ord. 33, r. 3
                  Keays v. Murdoch Magazines (U.K.) Ltd., C.A. [1991] 1 W.L.R. 1184

    Striking out
      Film broadcast and subsequent press reviews relied on as republication—Extent of liability
      of original publisher—Whether press reviews relevant to assessment oi general damages—
      Whether damage too remote—Whether justification for striking out republication
      allegation
            Slipper v. British Broadcasting Corpn., C.A. [1991] 1 Q.B. 283; [1990] 3 W.L.R. 967

DISCRIMINATION, RACE
  Army
    Discriminatory act
      Soldier formally complaining of racial discrimination—Redress refusec—Appeal to Army
      Board—No formal hearing of complaint—Evidence before boarc not disclosed to
      soldier—Board refusing redress for grievance—Whether procedure fa.r—Whether soldier
      entitled to compensation—Race Relations Act 1976, ss. 4, 75(8)(9,—Army Act 1955,
      s. 181(3) (as amended by Armed Forces Act 1971, s. 66(2))
            Reg. v. Army Board of the Defence Council, *Ex parte* Anderson,
                    D.C. [1992] Q.B. 169; [1991] 3 W.L.R. 4.2; [1991] I.C.R. 537

  Employment
    Applicant for employment
      Onus of proof—Applicant fulfilling employer's stated criteria not selected for interview—
      Tribunal requiring employers to explain failure to invite applicant for interview—Whether
      tribunal entitled to infer racial discrimination
                  King v. Great Britain-China Centre, C.A. [1992] I.C.R. 516

      Onus of proof—Industrial tribunal drawing inference of unlawful discrimination—Whether
      burden on respondent to disprove discrimination—Tribunal's recommendation that
      employers appoint applicant to next suitable vacancy—Whether recommendation ultra
      vires—Race Relations Act 1976, ss. 1(1)(a), 4(2)(b), 56(1)(c)
                    British Gas Plc. v. Sharma, E.A.T. [1991] I.C.R. 19

      Work permit—Indian national not requiring work permit—Employers requiring evidence of
      right to work—No such requirement for E.E.C. nationals—Comparisoi between applicant
      and E.E.C. nationals—Whether comparison of like with like—-Whether unlawful
      discrimination—Race Relations Act 1976, ss. 1(1)(a), 3(4)
            Dhatt v. McDonalds Hamburgers Ltd., C.A. [1991] 1 W.L.R. 527; [1991] I.C.R. 238

    Discriminatory act
      Time when act committed—Bank employees' prior service in Africa not to count
      in calculating pension entitlement—Complaints of unlawful discrimination—Whether
      complaints presented within three months of act of discrimination—Whether exclusion of
      prior service "deliberate omission" or "act extending over a period"— Race Relations Act
      1976, ss. 4(2), 68(1)(7), 78(1)   **Barclays Bank Plc. v. Kapur,** E.A.T. [1989] I.C.R. 142
                                     C.A. [1989] I.C.R. 753
            H.L.(E.) [1991] 2 A.C. 355; [1991] 2 W.L.R. 401; [1991] I.C.R. 208

'The Law Reports Index'

interpret and otherwise consider statutes and statutory instruments. It is important to know that the Daily Law Reports Index only gives you cases reported in *The Times*, the *Financial Times*, the *Independent* and *The Guardian* – but you need not turn to the newspapers themselves as the Index reproduces the cases reported in them.

A great many libraries have The Daily Law Reports Index on computer now. All you need to do is tap in the subject of your choice and the computer will refer you to all the newspaper reports on that subject. Of course it is usually only those cases mentioned in the last three or four months which will be of use, as most of those mentioned before then will probably have been reported in one of the law reporters. If that is the case the computer index or the most recent Law Report Index edition should tell you – check the list of cases reported in the front. You should never use a newspaper report when a full report may be available – they are very short and can occasionally be misunderstood.

To ensure there is no relevant case which has been decided in the month, you will need to look through the law reports of the newspapers themselves. This is because The Daily Law Reports Index, whether on computer or in binder form will not be completely up-to-date. Most law libraries cut out the law reports each day and add them to binders. There will be a separate one for *The Times*, the *Financial Times*, the *Independent* and *The Guardian*. It should only take you ten to fifteen minutes to check *The Times* and the *Independent*, less time to check the other two, and you may find something which proves to be invaluable. If you are in a desperate hurry, just check *The Times*.

4 Finding cases by subject matter

When there is no legislation involved in your case – your background resource should tell you whether or not this is so – you will need to find relevant cases according to the subject matter of your legal problem. Your background resource will refer you to plenty of cases, but it may not answer a particular point. Alternatively, there may not be a background resource which covers your question, or if there is one it is not sufficiently up-to-date.

In these circumstances you should start by checking Halsbury's Laws of England. Halsbury's has been referred to previously. It consists of fifty-plus volumes arranged alphabetically by subject matter, with yearly supplements to update the researcher, and monthly editions to inform you of the most recent case law and legislation. Use the index, to be found in two separate volumes, to refer you to the volume you need to consider your subject area. The indexes are quite specific and so it will refer you to particular paragraphs in particular volumes. These paragraphs will give you a commentary on the law as well as citing cases and referring you to relevant legislation. The commentary makes Halsbury's particularly useful, and many advocates use this commentary as a statement of the law in court.

Halsbury's covers every legal area you could think of and certain subjects which may not be the subject of any particular background resource. For example you can find the law on friendly societies, clubs, declarations and find information on ecclesiastical law.

If Halsbury's doesn't give you everything you need or you just want to check another research source, try The Law Reports Index, and Current Law's yearbooks and monthly editions, both mentioned earlier. Both these publications give summaries of cases as well as their citations for any of the law reporters in which they may have been reported. The summaries are arranged according to subject matter, the subjects being arranged alphabetically.

Note Never be content with the discovery of one case you think is relevant. You cannot move onto the next stage without a few cases, as when you try to update your research you may find that the one case you have has not been referred to since despite there being other relevant cases reported. Also when checking for cases under subject headings, eg in The Law Reports Index, never look under just one heading – try at least three. It is important to think laterally. For example, if your case involves judicial review of a decision of a local education authority, look under 'Judicial Review'; Local Government' and 'Education'.

C   The Next Step

Once you do find a useful case that is not the end of it. It is at this
point that your research efforts can become very productive. Once
you have found a few relevant cases you have the key to all other
relevant case law. Your research can be expanded by using two basic
tools – The Law Reports Index and Current Law's Case Citator.
Theses tools are discussed in the next chapter.

REVIEW

Questions

1 In what volume of which reporter will you find the case of *R v Sang* (1979) 69 Cr App . 282?

2 Who is making the application for judicial review in the case of *R v Kent County Council, ex p Daniels*?

3 When was the case of *R v Bow Street Stipendiary Magistrate, ex p DPP* (1990) 91 Cr App R 283 decided?

4 Who is the plaintiff in the case of *D & C Builders Ltd. v Rees* [1965] 3 All ER 837? Who is the defendant?

5 How can a background resource lead you to a relevant case?

6 Is it worth reading the headnotes in a case report?

7 Once you have found a relevant statute or statutory instrument, where do you look to find a case which considers them?

8 If there is no legislation involved in your research problem, where do you look to find your first group of cases?

9 How do you find relevant cases which may have been decided in the last year?

10 Where do you find relevant cases which way have been decided in the last month?

Answers

1 Volume 69 of the Criminal Appeal Reports.

2 The applicant in this case is Daniels – he is applying for judicial review by the court of a decision of the Kent County Council, which affects him.

3 This case was in fact decided in 1989 – the date given in the citation is the date the case is reported. There can often be a long delay before the case is properly reported.

Check the report itself which will give a date the judgment was handed down by the court – you'll find it under the name of the case on the first page.

4   The plaintiff is the company, D & C Builders Limited; the defendant is the individual, Rees.

5   Most background resources are littered with footnotes to the commentary – many will be citations for cases which the author views as authority for a certain proposition. But it is good not to rely on the author's view – check the case out yourself.

6   It is worth reading headnotes to get a quick grasp of the issues in the case and the judgment given. This will tell you if the case is relevant. However, you should never rely on headnotes if you wish to rely on the case as they are the creation of the publisher. Check the main judgment.

7   Once you have worked out what part of the statute or statutory instrument is relevant, check the Law Reports Index or the Current Law Legislation Citator. In these publications the statutes or S.I.s are arranged chronologically, and, within each year, alphabetically. They will refer you to the cases which have considered or interpreted the legislation.

8   Check The Law Reports Index and the Current Law Yearbooks under the subject heading which best refers to your research area. Always try more than one subject heading – try to think laterally.

9   Check the Current Law monthly editions, under the subject heading which best covers your research area. Also check The Daily Law Reports Index, in paperback and on computer.

10 Check the daily newspaper law reports for the last month. You will find them in *The Times*, the *Financial Times*, the *Independent* and *The Guardian*.

Chapter 9

Citators and Indexes: Expand and Update your Research

Once you have found a few cases which you feel are relevant to the legal question you require answering, you must not stop there. For one thing you must check that the cases you do have are still good law. Secondly, you should expand on the case law you have. This chapter shows you how.

A   The Current Law Case Citator

This is in another in the Current Law series. It can be found in blue hardback editions. There is one edition for 1947-1976; another for 1977-1988; and paperbacks for the years since 1988.

The Case Citator lists all cases which have been digested, distinguished, followed or overruled in the years covered by the particular edition. All you need to do is look in the alphabetical list for the names of the cases you already have. For example, if your original case is *R v Alladice* (1966), you should look down the alphabetical list. If it is mentioned, the citator will refer you to other cases, with their citations, and tell you if those other cases digest, distinguish, overrule or follow your original case of *Alladice*.

B   The Law Reports Index

The Law Reports Index is produced in red hardback, with pink paperbacks to provide the researcher with the latest cases. The paperback editions are produced about every three months.

As explained in the last chapter, the Index is arranged by subject area. But the Index also contains a list of cases at the back, under the heading 'cases judicially considered' arranged alphabetically. This list, if it contains one of your cases will refer you to other cases which have followed, considered, overruled and distinguished your cases.

For example, if you look in the Index for 1971-1980, and find your case of *R v Alladice* (1966) mentioned in the list at the back, it will refer you to cases reported between 1971 and 1980 which mention *R v Alladice*.

Never just check the 1971-1980 hardback edition, of course—check the 1961-1970 and the 1981-1990 editions. Always ensure that any case you find has not been overruled since. Finally, look at the paperbacks which follow the 1981-1990 hardback, including the very latest one. These should tell you of any relevant cases reported recently; however, they will not give you the very latest cases.

Once you have your list of new cases you should look at their full reports and ensure that they have in fact mentioned your original case. Consider how that case has been dealt with. Look at the list of authorities in the reports and check out the cases mentioned there as well.

It is important to note that the Index will only refer you to cases in the more major law reporters, that is, The Weekly Law Reports; The Queen's Bench Reports; The Chancery Division Report; The Family Division Reports; The Appeal Cases Reports; The All England Law Reports; The Industrial Cases Reports (ICR); The Lloyd's Law Reports; The Road Traffic Reports; The Local Government Reports and The Criminal Appeal Reports.

C   The Daily Law Reports Index

The Daily Law Reports Index is produced in paper form and computer form.

The paper version can be found in large red hardbacks. Each edition covers one year, with red paperback updates produced approximately once every three months. Added to this is a final binder which includes the most recent cases reported in the last few months.

The editions include summaries of cases reported in the daily newspapers and the daily newspapers alone. The summaries are arranged throughout the publication alphabetically by the name of the case. At the back is a list of statutes and statutory instruments which have been considered by the cases summarised in that particular edition. There is also an alphabetical list of cases referred to in the cases summarised.

In order to help you find a case specifically on the point, The Daily Law Reports Index has the summaries separately produced under different subject headings.

The computerised Daily Law Reports Index usually holds all cases which have been reported in the daily newspapers in the last five or six years. It will usually give you the law reporter citation if the case has been propertly reported since. In order to use the computerised Daily Law Reports Index, you merely enter a subject name and the computer will tell you how many cases it holds in that particular area. It will then give you a list of the case names, with the most recent case first, going backwards in time. The citation will be for one or more of the newspapers. Fortunately, the computer, like the paper version, does give you summaries of the cases listed. You just need to press 'return' with the case cited and the computer will provide you with a brief summary. This at least will enable you to sort the wheat from the chaff. But you should write down the names and check them out in the binders in the library which hold the newspaper reports, as there you will find a longer summary. This can be a little tedious, and is made more difficult when the computer produces 23 relevant case names under the heading, 'mortgages'!

When the computer does produce a large number of case names don't despair. Try typing in 'mortgages' and 'fraud' under Words and Phrases to cut down the number of relevant cases.

For the cases which have been reported in the newspapers in the last month you will need to look at the newspaper cut-outs themselves, as neither version of The Daily Law Reports Index will be completely up-to-date.

D   Other Means of Updating and Expanding your Research

1 Halsbury's Laws of England

Halsbury's Laws is arranged in brown hardback volumes, alphabetically according to subject matter. These volumes are often rather out of date, but there are hardback supplementary volumes. The supplementary volumes are a little annoying because you need to know the relevant paragraph(s) in the original volume in order to follow the updates in the supplements. However, what are quite useful are the monthly editions of Halsbury's Laws. These are paperbacks which are usually to be found in a binder. In these you will find new case law summarised under the different subject headings. The summaries are followed by the citation for the case – including the newspaper citation if it has not yet been fully reported.

2 Current Law

The Current Law Yearbooks are blue hardbacks produced, fairly obviously, each year. Each has a list of cases which have been considered in cases reported in that particular year. The Yearbooks also contain case summaries of cases decided in that year, and a helpful subject index at the back.

Current Law also has monthly paperback editions, called the 'Monthly Digest', which include case summaries of the latest cases, with citations. The summaries are to be found under alphabetically arranged subject headings. There is a useful subject index in the back, and a list of the subject headings used throughout the digest at the front (see pages 141-143 below).

The Current Law Monthly Digest also a list of Statutes and statutory instruments referred to in the cases summarised in that particular edition. The Digest also includes a separate section on commencement dates of statutes, where the commencement takes place that month, in the same way as the Yearbooks.

EASEMENTS AND PRESCRIPTION

143. Right of way—dispute—plan attached to conveyance—whether to be used to establish intention of parties

S was the owner of woodland fronting on to a drive which ran out into a public road. He sought to erect a house on the land but was opposed by L, the owner of the drive, who claimed that S's only right of way over the drive was for the purposes of using his land as woodland. No express right of way had been reserved on conveyance of the land in 1955. At first instance, S was granted a declaration that he was entitled to use the drive for the purposes of building and using a house on his land.

Held, dismissing L's appeal, that the law would imply the grant of an easement necessary to give effect to the intention of the parties, provided that it could be established that the parties had intended that the subject of the grant should be used in some definite and particular manner. In the absence of other evidence it was proper to look at the plan attached to the conveyance to establish the definite and particular use intended and it was enough if this was established on a balance of probabilities. According to the plan, houses had been built on adjoining plots at the date of the grant in 1955 which led to the assumption that such was the intention here (*Pwlbach Colliery* v. *Woodman* [1915] A.C. 634 applied).

STAFFORD v. LEE [1992] NPC 141, C.A.

144. Right of way—motorvehicles—restrictions—whether dictated by size and nature of the track

A right of way over a track with motorvehicles was restricted as to the nature and frequency of the motorvehicles by the size and nature of the track itself (*Todrick* v. *Western National Omnibus Co.* [1934] Ch. 561, *Ballard* v. *Dyson* (1808) 1 Taunt 285, *Keefe* v. *Amor* [1964] C.L.Y. 1207 considered).

WHITE v. RICHARDS, *The Times*, March 22, 1993, C.A.

145. Right to use—sewer—sewer ruptured by servient owner—dominant owner installing faulty system—whether liable in nuisance

Building by R caused a sewer, over which T had an easement, to rupture. T remedied the matter, after ineffective works by R, and obtained the cost of the works from R. Faults appeared in the system causing nuisance to R.

Held, that the action for nuisance failed as R was the author of the nuisance. T's actions constituted a reasonable attempt to solve the problem caused by R and did not break the chain of causation.

ROBINS v. TUPMAN [1992] NPC 135, C.A.

EDUCATION

146. Higher education corporations

EDUCATION (HIGHER EDUCATION CORPORATIONS) (WALES) (NO. 3) ORDER 1993 (No. 56) [65p], made under the Education Reform Act 1988 (c.40), ss.122, 123(4), 126(2); operative on February 5, 1993; provides for the establishment of a body corporate to operate the North East Wales Institute of Higher Education.

EDUCATION

147. Judicial review—Education Secretary's decision—closure of grammar schools—whether application appropriate in the circumstances. See R. v. SECRETARY OF STATE FOR EDUCATION, *ex p.* BANHAM, §2.

148. Local education authority—duty of care to children with special educational needs—whether authority liable for sexual assault by headmaster of special school. See PALMER v. HARROW LONDON BOROUGH, §298.

149. Special educational needs—transport—considerable journey to special school—whether statement of needs should specify maximum journey time

[Education Act 1944 (c.31), s.55(1); Education Act 1981 (c.60), ss.1, 5, 7(1)(2) (as amended), Sched. 1, para. 3; Education (Special Educational Needs) Regulations 1983 (S.I. 1983 No. 29), reg. 10(1)(c) (as amended).]

There was no obligation for a local authority to specify a maximum journey time in a statement for a child with special needs, merely the general nature of the transport provision made.

P, child with special needs, was at a special school, the journey to which took one hour and during which, because of his condition, he had to be strapped in. The statement of his special educational needs listed under "additional educational provision" mentioned "provision of transport from home to school and return." His parents contended that "a maximum journey time of 45 minutes" should be added and when the local authority declined to do so, P applied for judicial review, submitting that the relevant statutory provisions required the addition of the words, alternatively that the decision to omit was so unreasonable no local authority could have refused to add them.

Held, dismissing the application, that the provision of non-stressful transport was a non-educational provision which had to be specified in the statement of special educational needs, although there was no statutory requirement to set out the full terms and conditions under which the provision was to be made available; it was sufficient to specify the general nature of the provision rather than a maximum journey time. Significantly longer journey times were regarded as acceptable for pupils attending special schools than for those attending ordinary schools and in the present case the journey time did not render P unable to benefit from the school. The decision was not so unreasonable that no authority could reasonably have made it.

R. v. HEREFORD AND WORCESTER COUNTY COUNCIL, *ex p.* P. [1992] 2 FLR 207, McCullough J.

150. Teachers' boycott of national curriculum—whether trade dispute. See WANDSWORTH LONDON BOROUGH COUNCIL v. NATIONAL ASSOCIATION OF SCHOOL MASTERS AND WOMEN TEACHERS, §395.

151. Training grants

EDUCATION (TRAINING GRANTS) REGULATIONS 1993 (No. 72) [£1·55], made under the Education (No. 2) Act 1986 (c.6), ss.50, 63; operative on February 15, 1993; consolidate with amendments S.I. 1990 No. 1857.

152. Articles

Children Act 1989: the education provisions *(Dr N. Harris)*: [1992] Ed.Law 61.
Employment of school teachers by education authorities in Scotland *(G. McPherson)*: [1992] Ed.Law 173.
Exclusion of pupils: is it the most appropriate way of dealing with indiscipline? *(D. Sasson)*: [1992] Ed.Law 55.
Further and Higher Education Act 1992—the end of the binary line *(N. Bastin)*: [1992] Ed.Law 163.

Local complaints procedures under the Education Reform Act 1988 *(N. Harris)*: [1993] 1 J.S.W.L. 19.
Maastricht agreement and education: one step forward, two steps back? *(C. Barnard)*: [1992] Ed.Law 123.
National Curriculum assessments arrangements—the legal minimum *(D. William)*: [1992] Ed.Law 135.
Quality control and accountability to the consumer: and evaluation of the Education (Schools) Act 1992 *(Dr N. Harris)*: [1992] Ed.Law 109.
School teachers' pay and conditions: the new legislative framework *(D. Morris)*: [1992] Ed.Law 19.

153. Books

Lowe, Chris—The School Governor's Legal Guide. Paperback. ISBN 1–85524–200–1. Croner Publications.

ELECTION LAW

154. Parliamentary constituencies—Wales

PARLIAMENTARY CONSTITUENCIES (WALES) (MISCELLANEOUS CHANGES) ORDER 1993 (No. 227) [£1·10], made under the Parliamentary Constituencies Act 1986 (c.56), s.4; operative on February 23, 1993; gives effect to a report by the Boundary Commission for Wales.

EMPLOYMENT

155. Grievance procedure—public interest immunity—whether internal police grievance procedure generated public interest immunity

Statements made during the course of the Metropolitan Police grievance procedure were not protected by public interest immunity.
COMMISSIONER OF POLICE OF THE METROPOLIS *v.* LOCKER, *The Times*, March 16, 1993, E.A.T.

156. Industrial tribunal—jurisdiction—deduction of pay—half-day of industrial action—whether covered by industrial tribunal

[Wages Act 1986 (c.48), s.1(5)(e).]
The jurisdiction of the industrial tribunal did not extend to the deduction of a whole-day's pay for half-a-day's industrial action, under s.1(5)(e) of the Wages Act 1986, as there was no dispute as to the amount of wages deducted or as to the industrial action.
SUNDERLAND POLYTECHNIC *v.* EVANS, *The Times*, March 16, 1993, E.A.T.

157. Racial discrimination—doctor—refusal of full registration by General Medical Council—whether industrial tribunal having jurisdiction to hear complaint

[Medical Act 1983 (c.54), s.29.]
A doctor cannot bring a complaint of racial discrimination to an industrial tribunal in respect of a refusal by the General Medical Council to grant full registration, as he had a right of review under s.29 of the Medical Act 1983 which was in the nature of an appeal (*R. v. Army Board of the Defence Council, ex p. Anderson* [1991] C.L.Y. 13 distinguished).
KHAN *v.* GENERAL MEDICAL COUNCIL, *The Independent*, March 24, 1993, E.A.T.

'Current Law Monthly Digest'

The Digests have the cases arranged in four sections - the law for England and Wales; the law for Scotland; the law for Northern Ireland and the law of the European Communities.

3 Law reporters

Sometimes you will need to look for cases not covered by The Law Reports Index, or The Daily Law Reports Index—that is, cases reported in the less well-known law reporters, such as British Company Cases; Industrial Relations Law Reports; Immigration Appeal Reports; and The Criminal Law Review. If so, check Current Law or the cases index of the Empire and English Digest which cites cases reported in a wider variety of law reporters.

If your legal research area is covered by a particular law reporter which is not covered by the Indexes or Current Law, there is nothing wrong with looking at the law reporters themselves. Most reporters have cumulative indexes which cover a set number of years. These indexes provide a list of case names, as well as a subject index in the majority of cases. Make sure you look for the cumulative index first - don't go wondering through each and every index of each and every volume of the reporter.

REVIEW

Questions

1 Where will the researcher find the most up-to-date cases?

2 What publications does Current Law produce and what are their uses?

3 What publications give brief summaries of reported cases under different subject headings?

4 Which publication has the most comprehensive list of reported cases?

5 What will computer indexes usually give you?

Answers

1 In the law reports produced in *The Times* and the *Independent.* The Daily Law Reports Index on file and on computer produces the same reports, but they are usually a few weeks out of date.

2 a) Current Law Yearbooks - include case summaries under subject headings with a case citator and legislation citator available.

b) Current Law Monthly Digests - for the current year, which include the same material as the yearbooks.

c) Current Law Case Citator.

d) Current Law Legislation Citator - for statutes and statutory instruments.

Current Law cites cases from a wider range of law reporters, including the newspapers.

3 Current Law Yearbook and monthly digests; the Empire and English Digest and the Law Reports and Daily Law Reports Indexes.

4 The Empire and English Digest, which includes Commonwealth cases.

5   Cases reported in the newspapers (with the law reporter
     citation if it has been properly reported since); and an
     index of articles produced in most legal journals. Also
     statutory law.

Chapter 10

How to Write a Legal Memorandum

Do the words 'legal memorandum' conjure up images of dusty desks, granny glasses, and massive leather-bound tomes at least two inches thick? If so, your first step is to relax and forget all such notions. A legal memorandum can be a couple of paragraphs long. Whether you are doing research for yourself or for another, the main purpose of a memo is to force you to put the results of your research in writing.

A   Why Prepare a Legal Memorandum?

Why is this important? For three basic reasons. The first is that you will not really know whether your research is done until you try to write it up. Most people have undoubtedly had the experience of thinking they understood something until the moment they put pen to paper. The same is true of legal research. You may think you have answered the question you started out with, but you cannot be sure until it appears in black and white. Although you may believe that the formal structure for the memorandum suggested here is unnecessary for this purpose, it does serve as a checklist for your research. Later, as you become more proficient, you may wish to adopt a more informal way of checking your results.

The second primary function of a legal memorandum is to provide you with an accessible record of the fruits of your research after time has erased the memories from your mind. It is common for people to put in a day or two of research in the law library on a particular issue, neglect to take an extra hour or two to write it up, and later have to spend another day in the library because they are unable to reconstruct what they found from their notes.

The third primary function of a legal memorandum is to communicate the results of your research to someone else. This will be necessary if you are a legal assistant doing research for a supervising lawyer.

B   How to Prepare a Legal Memorandum

In this section we tell you how to prepare a legal memorandum. Obviously this is a skill which requires a lot of practice. As a follow-up, we suggest that you do at least one of the research hypotheticals in the appendices (if the necessary materials are available in your law library) and prepare a memorandum based on your work. Then compare your memorandum with the one accompanying the hypothetical. If you are able to do all of the exercises, your writing skills will get even better.

1 Overview

In Chapter 7, we stated that judicial opinions almost always have four primary elements:

- a statement of the facts
- a statement of the issue or issues
- a decision or holding on the issue or issues, and
- a discussion of the reasoning underlying the holding.

We also pointed out that these elements do not necessarily appear in any particular order. Like case opinions, legal memoranda should include a statement of the facts, a statement of the issue or issues, a conclusion about what the law is (equivalent to the holding), and a brief discussion of why you reached your conclusion. Also, like judicial opinions, it is useful to put these items in this particular order.

2 Internal consistency

The main idea is to structure your legal memorandum so that it is internally consistent. For example, you should include enough relevant facts in the memo for your statement of the issue to make sense. If your issue is whether a new owner of a house can evict a tenant for having pets even though the prior landlord allowed them, your statement of facts would have to include such items as:

- the date ownership was transferred
- information about any rental agreement or lease that was executed by the tenant, and so on.

In a similar way, your discussion of the reasoning that you use to arrive at your conclusion has to include cases or statutes that are relevant to the facts that you have listed in the memo. If your law sources and facts do not match up on some level, your reasoning is faulty.

C   Sample Legal Memorandum

Now let us look at a sample of a legal memorandum. While the memoranda that you produce may be different in format, it will not hurt to keep the following checklist in your head:

- Did I put down all facts that are relevant to my legal issue as stated, and to my legal conclusions?
- Did I state the legal issue clearly?
- Did I arrive at a definitive conclusion about the legal issue as applied to my facts?
- Did I state clearly the reasons for my conclusion while presenting all sides of the legal picture?
- Did I support my conclusions with primary legal authority?

SAMPLE MEMORANDUM

To: Ruth Rawlinson

From: Terry Jacobs

Topic: False imprisonment and malicious prosecution in the case of Harry Powell

Facts

The plaintiff was convicted of theft on the 30 January, 1989. He was arrested for that offence by DC Allan and PC Taylor on 23 May 1988 at 10.05, and taken to the Stoke Railton Police Station in London W14.

The plaintiff (P) was cautioned upon arrest and his detention was authorised at 10.34 upon arrival at the police station.

P was first interviewed at 14.24 on the 23 May 1988, by DC Booth and DC Fowler. This interview was not tape recorded, but written down. It lasted for two-and-a-half hours. The written interview contains a confession to the theft, but the P denies that he made such a confession – he says these particular words are not his.

P was asked to sign each page of the written interview, which was read back to him. However, P states that he was asked to sign a blank page at the end. He says he was told this was to be used to list his previous convictions.

P's custody record states that his continued detention was first authorised at 22.16 on 23 May, by DI Jarver.

P was eventually charged with theft at 1.10 on 24 May. He was refused police bail, and was kept in custody until being brought before Harrow Magistrates on the morning of 26 May.

The Harrow Magistrates refused to allow P to be bailed, ostensibly because of a previous refusal to answer bail in 1986.

P was kept in custody until his Crown Court trial on 30 January 1989. He pleaded not guilty, but there he was convicted of theft and sentenced to nine months imprisonment. Effectively that meant he was free to go once the trial ended.

The only real evidence against P was the alleged confession he made on 23 May. In court P denied he had made the confession, but the jury clearly did not believe him.

P appealed against his conviction on the basis of the fabricated confession. As the result of an ESDA test, it was shown by one of P's experts that one of the pages in the interview had been added later. This was the page on which the words of the confession could be found. His conviction was overturned as being unsafe and unsatisfactory. The Court of Appeal accepted that there was a possibility that the confession had been fabricated.

Now P wishes to bring an action for false imprisonment and malicious prosecution against the Metropolitan Police.

Issues

Does P have an action in false imprisonment and malicious prosecution. What are his likely damages? How is the fabricated confession relevant? Is the authorisation of detention relevant? What is the effect of the Magistrates' decision to refuse bail?

Conclusion

P has an action in false imprisonment and malicious prosecution as the fabrication of the confession could be used to show lack of reasonable cause and the requisite malice.

The authorisation of detention while P was in the police station took place long after it should have done and so is relevant to the issue of false imprisonment.

The fact that the magistrates refused bail reduces the damages for false imprisonment, but does not affect the major claim of malicious prosecution as P would not have been prosecuted had it not been for the fabricated confession.

Reasoning

a) False Imprisonment

As to the initial detention, the custody officer can authorise detention without charge, if he has reasonable grounds for believing that detention is necessary for one of the two reasons listed in section 37(2) of The Police And Criminal Evidence Act 1984 (PACE). The custody record of P records that he was detained at 10.34 to obtain evidence from him, by questioning. This reason is rather difficult to refute, and, at this stage in P's custody, I do not believe his detention would be regarded as false imprisonment.

As for the next authorisation, this was given by DI Jarver at 22.16. P's custody record shows he was further detained in order to obtain further evidence by questioning. This review was carried out by a DI, as necessary under section 40(1)(b) of PACE; but he also needed to be independent of the investigation. On the facts now available it is difficult to say whether or not this is so. As for the reason for the further detention, it is a valid reason under section 40(8) of PACE. Whether or not this is a true reason is for the defendant, ie the Metropolitan Police, to prove. It is unlikely to be true if P had already confessed by the crime. What more did the police need to ask? In fact they did not ask P anything more after that one interview.

The review at 22.16 was very late. Under section 40(3)(a) of PACE, the first review is meant to take place six hours after the detention was first authorised, that is, six hours after 1034. The review was in fact nearly 12 hours after the initial detention. There is an excuse available to police officers under section 40(4), that is that it was not practicable to authorise detention any earlier. The police must be put to strict proof of this. The burden of proof is on them.

If it is found that the review at 22.16 was invalid this makes the detention of P unlawful, probably as from six hours after the first detention, or thereabouts. The breach of PACE would also allow P to bring an action for breach of statutory duty by the Metropolitan Police.

b) Malicious Prosecution

For an action in malicious prosecution to lie there must have been a prosecution, which is clear here, and a termination of the prosecution in the P's favour - which has occurred here with the overturning of P's conviction by The Court of Appeal - *Herniman v Smith* [1938] AC 305, 315. P must further show a lack of reasonable and probable cause, and that the proposed defendant (D) acted maliciously.

There are two questions to be asked:

(1) Did D honestly believe that a charge against P was warranted? This is a subjective test.

(2) Was D's belief in (1) based on reasonable grounds? This is an objective test.

The jury will have to consider what was in the mind of the police officers who interviewed P. If the court accepts that the confession was fabricated it will be very easy to show lack of reasonable cause. The officer who eventually charged P must have relied on the fabricated confession as there was no other evidence.

As for malice, any motive other than that of simply instituting a prosecution for the purpose of bringing a person to justice, is a malicious motive on the part of the prosecutor - *Stevens v Midland Counties Rly* (1854) 10 Ex. 352. What was the motive for P's prosecution in this case by the police? The motive was not one of justice - which can clearly be inferred from the fact of the fabricated confession.

c) Damages

For the false imprisonment, the average hourly rate is about £250, depending on how long the detainee was detained. In P's case, £250 is too high a rate as he was detained for quite some time before appearing in front of the Magistrates on Monday morning. A better rate would be £60 per hour, giving him damages of approximately £3,000.

As for the malicious prosecution, the general damages for this will be determined on a weekly or monthly scale, at possibly £3,000 per month, giving damages of £24,000. Added to this may be exemplary damages awarded against the police. This is highly likely in the present case as there has been a fabrication of a confession. There may be a reduction in damages due to the P's past, as the court may believe that due to this, his reputation has not been sullied by the experience.

Resources used

Clayton & Tomlinson - 'Civil Actions Against The Police'

Halsbury's Laws of England

Clerk and Lindsall on Torts

Michael Zander – 'The Police and Criminal Evidence Act 1984'

Halsbury's Statutes

REVIEW

Questions

1 Why write a legal memorandum?

2 What are the main elements of a legal memorandum?

3 How do I know when my memo is complete?

Answers

1 Because once you attempt to write down the answer to your legal problem you will see if there are any holes in your argument. Also, it will create a record of what you have researched and where. Thirdly, you will almost always need to communicate the results of your research to someone else.

2 Statement of the facts

Statement of the issues

Conclusion

Reasoning

Resources considered

3 Are all the relevant facts mentioned in the memo?

Are the legal issues state clearly?

Is my conclusion as definitive as possible with the present information?

Did I state the reasons for my conclusion clearly?

Have I mentioned the primary legal authority?

Chapter 11

The Legal Research Method: Examples

In Chapter 2, you were showed an overall method for undertaking a legal research project. And in each of the following chapters an important part of that method was explained. Now it is time to pull it all together in an example.

A   The Facts

Assume the following facts: Laura, a working single parent, has her child Amy in a day-care centre in London. When Laura picks Amy up at the end of the day, she notices a nasty bruise on Amy's temple. The teacher explains that Amy fell from the horizontal bar in the gym early in the morning, but has suffered no adverse symptoms. Although Laura is furious at not being informed of Amy's injury earlier, she does not confront the teacher. She does, however, take Amy to the emergency room of the local hospital. An X-ray discloses an internal haemorrhage. Amy is rushed into surgery, which lasts about two hours.

The surgery is a success, but the doctors are very critical of the delay in bringing Amy to the hospital and intimate that some brain damage may have occurred as a result. Fortunately, tests taken several weeks later show no brain damage, but in the meantime Laura has suffered extreme anxiety, has had trouble sleeping, and has experienced nightmares. Although Laura's psychological problems were intense, she suffered no physical symptoms.

Laura is very angry with the day-care centre for not realising the potential seriousness of the injury. She has been told by several people that she ought to see a lawyer. From her general knowledge of the law, Laura is pretty sure that Amy could sue the day-care centre for the consequences of the delay in seeking proper medical treatment; she is less sure whether she can recover money (damages) for her own emotional torment.

Before she sees a lawyer, Laura wants to do a little legal research for herself.

B   Classify the Problem

Following the suggestions made in Chapter 4, Putting your Questions into Legal Categories, Laura must:

- determine whether European, national or local law is involved;
- determine whether the matter is civil or criminal; and
- determine whether her research will involve procedural or substantive questions.

Since it is apparent that Laura's dispute with day-care centre involves a personal injury (Laura's emotional distress), and since most personal injury cases are controlled by national law (see Chapter 4), Laura would tentatively start with a national law classification. While the day-care centre might receive some local government money, the receipt of local funds by an independent or community entity would probably not transform Laura's dispute from a national to a local question unless her dispute had something to do with the funds themselves.

The next step is to determine that the matter is civil rather than criminal. Although there are times when an act violates both the criminal law and a civil duty owed to another person (failure to pay child support is an example, battery is another), this is not such a case.

Now that Laura has tentatively classified the problem as one involving national civil law, she needs to determine whether the question is substantive or procedural. In essence, Laura's question is whether she can recover damages for her torment. This type of question is really at the heart of the substantive law—that is, determining whether someone has done something wrong. But if she decides that the day-care centre has been legally negligent, she would then become interested in state civil procedural law—that is, how Laura's case gets into court and stays there until she recovers.

So Laura's next task is to determine under which civil substantive law category her problem falls. By skimming the list of substantive civil law topics in Chapter 4, she quickly narrows the issue down to 'torts'. Why? Because Laura suffered an injury—

emotional suffering—that was arguably caused by the day-care centre's failure promptly to obtain medical attention for Amy. Whether Laura can recover money for her suffering under the law of torts remains to be determined.

C   Select a Background Resource

Now that she has narrowed the issue—a national, civil, substantive, tort—Laura needs to select an appropriate legal background resource to supply an overview of the part of tort law that is relevant to her problem. Basically, Laura wants to find out whether the day-care centre has wronged her in some way—as opposed to Amy—and if so whether her injury qualifies for damages. Finally, she wants to know what she must show to prove her case. For example, is her testimony enough, or does she need doctor's reports?

A good background resource would be Clerk and Lindsell on Torts (see pages 164–167).

D   Use the Index

Now that Laura has selected a background resource for her project, she needs to deal with the index. This involves writing down as many words and phrases as she can think of that relate to her specific fact situation. (See Chapter 4, Putting your Questions into Legal Categories, section B.) Some of these might be:

- emotional distress
- emotional upset
- emotional suffering
- mental suffering
- negligence
- carelessness
- injury
- child

- parent and child
- anxiety
- damages
- shock/nervous shock
- fright
- sleeplessness
- nightmares
- post-traumatic stress disorder
- mental disorder

Index to 'Clerk & Lindsell on Torts'

Index to 'Clerk & Lindsell on Torts'

INDEX

Index to 'Clerk & Lindsell on Torts'

While Laura might get confused at this point (it is here that a law school education would probably pay off a little) and start reading some of these discussions, she would soon decide that her case probably does not qualify for 'intentional' infliction of emotional distress. While the day-care centre may have been impermissibly careless, they in no way 'intended' to cause Laura the anxiety or hurt Amy.

In fact, by again consulting the list of civil law topics in Chapter 4 (see the entry for torts), Laura determines that the day-care centre may have been negligent—that is, more careless than a hypothetical 'reasonable person' would have been under the circumstances. Once having determined that the emotional distress resulted from negligence rather than from an intentional act, Laura logically follows up on the entry 'Negligence', shown above.

E   Get an Overview of your Research Topic

Pages 169-174 contain an excerpt from Clerk and Lindsell of the actual discussion on negligent infliction of emotional distress and nervous shock. It shows that the emotional trauma must be causally linked to the physical injury. It must also be a medically recognised condition.

Laura would then turn to the supplements to Clerk and Lindsell (see pages 175-178). She would look at the same paragraphs in the supplements in order to ascertain whether or not the law has been expanded or overturned. It would not be enough to stop here as even the latest supplement will inevitably be a few months out of date. Hence the need to look at the latest edition of The Daily Law Reports Index and The Law Reports Index and the latest monthly editions of Current Law. She should check under 'Negligence', 'Education' and 'Damage'.

F   Use the Current Law Case Citator

As for case law, Laura should consider the cases of *De Franceschi v Storrier* (1989) 85 ALR 1 and *McLoughlin v O'Brian* [1983] AC 410

Nervous shock. Liability for this is now well established, but recognition came only gradually and the limits of it are still not altogether clear. If, as a result of nervous shock or terror the plaintiff suffers physically in health, damages for that physical injury are recoverable.[62] These are the cases which are labelled "shock" cases. It is important to distinguish them from situations where the defendant so startles a person that he suffers some immediate injury, e.g. by falling. Thus, in *Slatter v. British Railways Board*[63] goods wagons were shunted so violently into a stationary wagon, which the plaintiff was examining, that he was startled and fell, and his hand was cut off by the wagon. It was held that he could recover; but this is not a case of nervous shock.

Liability for shock has three aspects: first, the recognition of it as a kind of damage; secondly, whether there is a limit on the type of plaintiff who is entitled to recover; and thirdly, the special way in which the foreseeability of harm to the plaintiff has to be applied.

With regard to the first, liability was first recognised in cases in which it was inflicted wilfully or recklessly. So damages have been recovered for illness resulting from mental shock, where the defendant by way of a practical joke told the plaintiff that her husband had broken his leg in an accident,[64] and where a private detective in order to obtain inspection of certain letters informed the plaintiff that her fiancé was a German spy.[65]

Recognition of the careless infliction of shock came later,[66] and it is in this connection that a question arises as to how damage by shock should be viewed. There are two views, which may conveniently be labelled the "impact" and "shock" theories and which seem to correspond with two ways of regarding shock. One is that shock is only an extension of physical injury to the person, and this gives rise to the "impact theory" according to which, as long as it was reasonably foreseeable that the defendant's conduct would have inflicted injury on the plaintiff by actual impact of some sort, he can recover

---

[62] *Dulieu v. White* [1901] 2 K.B. 669; *Wilkinson v. Downton* [1897] 2 Q.B. 57; *Bell v. Great Northern Ry.* (1890) 26 L.R. Ir. 428; *Janvier v. Sweeney* [1919] 2 K.B. 316; *Hambrook v. Stokes Bros.* [1925] 1 K.B. 141. On the need for physical suffering see also *per* Mackinnon L.J. in *Owens v. Liverpool Corp.* [1939] 1 K.B. 394, 400; *per* Devlin J. in *Behrens v. Bertram Mills Circus Ltd.* [1957] 2 Q.B. 1. 28; *per* Paull J. in *Schneider v. Eisovitch* [1960] 2 Q.B. 430, 442. *Victorian Railway Commissioners v. Coultas* (1888) 13 App.Cas. 222 cannot be relied upon: *Coyle or Brown v. Watson* [1915] A.C. 1, 13, where a workman caught a chill bringing on pneumonia owning to the defendant's negligence, though there was no direct physical injury. The assumption that *Victoria Railway Commissioners v. Coultas, supra,* is not good law seems to have been accepted in *Bournhill v. Young* [1943] A.C. 92, and it was not followed by the Nova Scotia Supreme Court in *Horne v. New Glasgow* [1954] 1 D.L.R. 832. Another dubious decision is *Whitmore v. Euroway Express Coaches, The Times,* May 4, 1984; see *supra;* n. 59.

[63] (1966) 110 S.J. 688.

[64] *Wilkinson v. Downton* [1897] 2 Q.B. 57.

[65] *Janvier v. Sweeney* [1919] 2 K.B. 316.

[66] *Dulieu v. White* [1901] 2 K.B. 669; *Hambrook v. Stokes Bros* [1925] 1 K.B. 141.

Discussion of Nervous Shock: Clerk & Lindsell

for illness resulting from shock even though he sustained no injury from impact. There are a number of authorities which could be interpreted as supporting this view.[67] In *Bourhill v. Young*,[68] which is still one of the leading cases on shock, a negligent motor-cyclist killed himself in a collision with a third party. The plaintiff, who was pregnant, was at that moment alighting from a tramcar some distance away. She did not see the collision, but was startled by the noise, and later went to the spot and saw the blood. She alleged that she suffered shock and her baby was still-born. The House of Lords held that she had no action. Lords Thankerton, Russell and Macmillan appeared to follow the "impact" theory and held that she was outside the area of foreseeable impact and hence shock.[69] Her subsequent act in going to see the place was her own fault. The other view is that shock is a kind of damage on its own, and this gives rise to the "shock theory" according to which, as long as it was reasonably foreseeable that the defendant's conduct would have caused even only shock to an ordinarily strong-nerved person, situated in the position of the plaintiff, then the plaintiff can recover in respect of the shock to him. In *Bourhill* Lords Wright and Porter appeared to favour this.[70] "There can be no doubt," said Denning L.J., "that the test of liability for shock is foreseeability of injury by shock"[71]; and *Wagon Mound (No. 1)*[72] endorsed this view. Injury through shock is here treated as being different in kind from injury through impact, and it would seem that the "shock" theory now prevails. Shock is no longer a variant of bodily injury, but a separate kind of physical injury to the person.[73]

Even prior to *Wagon Mound (No. 1)*, the "shock" theory had been the basis of the decision in *Dooley v. Cammell Laird & Co. Ltd.*,[74] where a defective sling broke during loading operations on a ship and the goods dropped into the

---

[67] *Dulieu v. White* [1901] 2 K.B. 669, 675; *per* Sargant L.J. in *Hambrook v. Stokes Bros.*[1925] 1 K.B. 141, 162; *per* Singleton L.J. (adopting both "impact" and "shock" theories) and Hodson L.J. in *King v. Phillips* [1953] 1 Q.B. 429, 435, 443 (on which see Goodhart, 69 L.Q.R. 347); *Behrens v. Bertram Mills Circus Ltd.* [1957] 2 Q.B. 1. *Schneider v. Eisovitch* [1960] 2 Q.B. 430 is not strictly in point as the defendant admitted liability, so the court was not called upon to decide between the two theories. The plaintiff did come within the area of impact and was in fact so injured in addition to shock. (See on this case Jolowicz [1960] C.L.J. 156.) In other countries the "impact" theory prevailed in the following:- America: *Waube v. Warrington*, 216 Wis. 603 (1935); the American *Restatement of Torts*, Vol. 1, § 47, treats shock as a variant of physical injury; Canada: *Pollard v. Makarchuk* (1959) 16 D.L.R. (2d) 255; Australia: *Chester v. Waverley Municipal Council* (1939) 62 C.L.R. 1; South Africa: *Mulder v. South British Insurance Co. Ltd.* 1957 (2) S.A. 444.
[68] [1943] A.C. 92.
[69] *Ibid.* at pp. 98-99, 102-103, 105.
[70] *Ibid.* at pp. 108=109, 119.
[71] *King v. Phillips* [1953] 1 Q.B. 429, 441.
[72] [1961] A.C. 338, 426.
[73] *Abramzik v. Brenner* [1967] 65 D.L.R. (2d) 651; *cf. Vana V. Tosta* (1967) 66 D.L.R. (2d) 97.
[74] [1951] 1 Lloyd's Rep. 271 and see also *Carlin v. Helical Bar Ltd.* (1970) 9 K.I.R. 154. Other authorities: *Hambrook v. Stokes Bros.* [1925] 1 K.B. 141, where negligence was admitted in the

---

Discussion of Nervous Shock: Clerk & Lindsell

hold. The plaintiff, who was operating the crane and quite outside the area of injury to himself, suffered shock owing to his fear on account of the men working in the hold. It was held that he could recover. Since *Wagon Mound (No.1)* the cases have followed the "shock" theory. In *Boardman v. Sanderson (Keel and Block, Third Party)*[75] the plaintiff was paying a bill in the office of a garage when the defendant started to reverse the vehicle in which he was conveying the plaintiff and his infant son. In doing so he negligently ran over the boy's foot. The plaintiff did not see the occurrence, but heard his son scream and ran to assist. He suffered shock, and the Court of Appeal upheld the trial court's award of damages. The defendant knew that the plaintiff was within earshot and there was reasonable foreseeability of shock to him. In *Chadwick v. British Railways Board*[76] the plaintiff, who took part in rescue work after a railway collision due to the defendants' fault, suffered shock as a result of carrying out his ministrations amidst scenes of wreck and carnage. The defendants were held liable, since shock to a rescuer was foreseeable. In *Hinz v. Berry*[77] the plaintiff had left her husband and children in their car at a layby and was picking bluebells across the road when the defendant negligently ran into the car. The plaintiff heard the crash and turned round to see her husband and children lying injured, the former fatally. As a result of the shock she became ill, and the Court of Appeal upheld the trial court's award of damages. In *Carlin v. Helical Bar Ltd.*[78] a man was crushed to death by a crane owing to the fault of the defendants while the plaintiff was operating it. No fault attached to the latter. The shock had a serious and permanent effect on his personality, and he was awarded damages.

The second aspect of shock is not clear. The question is whether there is any limitation on the kind of person who is entitled to recover. Must he or she be related in some way to the injured party? Parents and husbands and wives are obviously entitled to recover.[79] Is it only these, or, if not, what other kinds

pleadings, so the court did not have to decide between the two theories. The importance of this admission was stressed by Atkin L.J. at pp. 152, 156; McNair J. in *King v. Phillips* [1952] 2 All E.R. 459, 461-462; Hodson L.J. on appeal in [1953] 1 Q.B. 429, 443-444. Opinions were expressed independently of the admission by Bankes L.J. [1925] 1 K.B. 141, 152, and Atkin L.J. at p. 157. See also *Currie v. Wardron* 1927 S.C. 538; *cf. Walker v. Pitlochry Motor Co.* 1930 S.C. 565; *Owens v. Liverpool Corp.* [1939] 1 K.B. 394; *per* Lords Wright and Porter in *Bourhill v. Young* [1943] A.C. 92, 108-109, 119; *per* Denning L.J. in *King v. Phillips* [1953] 1 Q.B. 429, 441-442.

[75] [1964] 1 W.L.R. 1317; on which see Dworkin (1962) 25 M.L.R. 353.

[76] [1967] 1 W.L.R. 912; *cf. Lawrence v. C.J. Evans (Properties)* (1965) 196 E.G. 407.

[77] [1970] 2 Q.B. 40; *Allen v. Dando* [1977] C.L.Y. 738.

[78] (1970) 9 K.I.R. 154. See also *Marshall v. Lionel Enterprises Inc.* (1971) 25 D.L.R. (3d) 141; *Benson v. Lee* [1972] V.R. 879.

[79] *Hambrook v. Stokes Brothers* [1925] 1 K.B. 141 (mother); *Boardman v. Sanderson (Keel and Block, Third Party)* [1964] 1 W.L.R. 1317 (father); *Kralj and Another v. McGrath and Another* [1986] 1 All E.R. 54 (mother); *Hinz v. Berry* [1970] 2 Q.B. 40 (wife and mother); *McLoughlin v. O'Brian and Others* [1983] A.C. 410 (wife and mother); *Jaensch v. Coffey* (1984) 54 A.L.R. 417 (wife).

Discussion of Nervous Shock: Clerk & Lindsell

of relationships will serve? In *Hambrook v. Stokes Brothers*[80] Bankes L.J. confined his remarks to "mothers," while Atkin L.J. did not. In *Boardman v. Sanderson (Keel and Block, Third Party)*[81] the Court of Appeal thought that near relatives could recover if they were within earshot and likely to come on the scene. It is submitted that the shock principle need not be confined to near relatives. The question is whether, on the particular facts, shock was reasonably foreseeable to the plaintiff as an ordinarily strong-nerved person. Near relationship is one factor in determining this, but not the only one. If in *Boardman* the plaintiff had been someone in charge of the boy, such as a nurse-maid or the father of a friend of the boy who was taking him out for the day, it would create an anomalous distinction to hold that such a person would not recover in such circumstances as those in which the boy's own father was held entitled to recover. In *Currie v. Wardrop*[82] damages were recovered by a fiancée. If a relationship of some kind there has to be, one would have to argue that in *Dooley v. Cammell Laird & Co. Ltd.*[83] there was a work-relationship between the plaintiff and his mates, who were put in danger. Stretching it further, would a rescue relationship serve; or, abandoning relationship altogether, would extremely harrowing circumstances suffice by themselves? Both features were present in *Chadwick v. British Railways Board*[84] where the plaintiff, a rescuer, was held entitled to recover for shock even though he was in no way related to the dead and injured whom he helped to rescue, but where he had to perform his acts of rescue in a horrifying situation. Whether a total stranger, not involved in any of the above ways, e.g. a bystander, could recover is uncertain, though there is no reason why he should not, provided that a strong nerved person similarly situated would have suffered shock.

Another point which has recently been established is that there can be recovery for shock through fear of injury to property as distinct from persons. The test of the reasonably strong-nerved person does not preclude recovery given suitable circumstances. The Court of Appeal so held in *Attia v. British Gas plc.*[85] where the plaintiff suffered shock on seeing her home being set on fire through the defendant's negligence, and she recovered damages. The point remains arguable in the case of a pet animal, though there seems to be no reason in principle why damages should not be awarded.[86] The question is whether, as a matter of policy, recovery for shock arising out

---

[80] [1925] 1 K.B. 141, 151-152, 157. *The Devonshire Maid* [1952] 2 Lloyd's Rep. 95, allowed recovery by a sister.
[81] [1964] 1 W.L.R. 1317.
[82] 1927, S.C. 538.
[83] [1951] 1 Lloyd's Rep. 271.
[84] [1967] 1 W.L.R. 912.
[85] [1988] Q.B. 304.
[86] *Davies v. Bennison* (1927) 22 Tas.L.R. 52 is not quite in point: damages for trespass included shock on seeing a pet cat killed; but this is explicable as parasitic damages, *infra*, § 10-163.

Discussion of Nervous Shock: Clerk & Lindsell

of damage to things should be allowed at all. *Owens v. Liverpool Corporation*[87] allowed relatives to recover for shock through fear for a corpse when a careless tram driver collided with the hearse. This case was criticised in *Bourhill v. Young,*[88] but it has to be remembered that it represents an application of the "shock" theory at a time when the "impact" theory was in the ascendant. Now that the "shock" theory prevails, it may well have been rehabilitated.

The third aspect of shock is that if the "shock" theory is adopted, the foreseeability test has to be applied subject to certain arbitrary limitations. When it is said that injury from shock has to be reasonably foreseeable, the test must be applied with reference to an ordinarily strong-nerved person. The question is whether such a person, situated where the plaintiff was, would have suffered shock. If yes, the plaintiff can recover, but not otherwise. "The question of liability," said Lord Wright,[89] "must generally depend on a normal standard of susceptibility"; and a little later, "generally, I think, a reasonably normal condition, if medical evidence is capable of defining it, would be the standard." Some such qualification as this is essential if "gold-digging" actions by hypersensitive and neurotic individuals are to be avoided.[90] Thus, a hypersensitive person will not recover for shock if in the circumstances a reasonably strong-nerved person would not have been shocked; but if even such a person would have been shocked, then a hypersensitive person may recover for the full extent of the shock produced by such sensitivity. In *Jaensch v. Coffey*[91] a wife, who saw her badly injured husband in hospital, developed a psychiatric illness and was held entitled to recover. Provided she was of normal fortitude, her predisposition to depression and anxiety was held to be no defence. As will be demonstrated later, a defendant has to take the victim *talem qualem;* foreseeability of shock only establishes initial liability, but given that there is liability for the full extent of the illness.[92]

Another limitation is that shock should result from what the plaintiff sees or hears first-hand, as distinct from what is reported. *Boardman's*[93] case shows

---

[87] [1939] 1 K.B. 394.

[88] [1943] A.C. 92.

[89] *Bourhill v. Young* [1943] A.C. 92, 110; *per* Lord Porter at p. 117. *Cf.* Paton: "The reasonable man is of fairly tough texture and he is entitled to assume that other members of the community are reasonably resilient in temperament": (1949) 23 A.L.J. 158, 161. The test was so applied in *Abramzik v. Brenner* (1967) 65 D.L.R. (2d) 651.

[90] "A wide field for imaginary claims": *Victoria Railway Commissioners v. Coultas* (1883) 13 App.Cas. 222, 226. This sentiment holds though the case itself has now been discredited.

[91] (1984) 54 A.L.R. 417; *Kralj v. McGrath* [1986] 1 All E.R. 54; *Brice v. Brown* [1984] 1 W.L.R. 997.

[92] More generally on this point, see *post*, §§ 10-151 *et seq.*:10-161.

[93] [1964] 1 W.L.R. 912. In *Guay v. Sun Publishing Co.* [1953] 4 D.L.R. 577, the plaintiff failed to recover for shock on reading a false report in a newspaper that her family had been killed. Much emphasis was placed in *Hambrook v. Stokes Bros.* [1925] 1 K.B. 141, 152, 159, 165, on the point that only what Mrs. Hambrook had seen herself was relevant to the question of liability for shock, not

Discussion of Nervous Shock: Clerk & Lindsell

that it is sufficient if the plaintiff hears the accident occurring, though he does not actually see it. What of the person who neither sees nor hears the occurrence, but who suffers shock by seeing the result later, *e.g.* the injured victim in hospital? In *McLoughlin v. O'Brian and Others*[94] the plaintiff, a mother, was at home when she was told that her family had been involved in a car accident. She went to the hospital and learned that her youngest child was dead, her elder daughter and son in a pitiable condition and her husband dazed. She sued the defendants for the shock she suffered. The Court of Appeal rejected her claim on policy grounds although the court admitted that there was foreseeability of shock to her. The House of Lords, reversing the decision, considered the policy arguments against liability and rejected their application in the present case. Their Lordships still insisted on proximity in time and space, but said that this is not confined to direct and immediate sight or hearing; it is sufficient if the sight or hearing takes place in the "immediate aftermath." The test is whether a strong-nerved person in the plaintiff's situation would have suffered shock. It is true that a person, who sees or hears the occurrence taking place, has no choice but to see or hear it, but a person who goes to see the victim in hospital acts of his or her own volition. Nevertheless, there is a distinction between one who acts under a legal or moral duty, e.g. a parent or relative,[95] and a stranger.[96] The question concerning sight or hearing through simultaneous television was left by the House for future consideration. The insistence on personal sight or hearing excludes liability for shock produced by a third party's information. Perhaps this refers to third-party information subsequent to the "immediate aftermath," for it seems unjust to exclude liability if such information is still part of the occurrence. The potential widening of liability, coupled with the uncertainty resulting from the case-by-case approach advocated by the House, leaves some questions to be clarified.

---

what she had been told by bystanders. The utterance of Paull J. in *Scneider v. Eisovitch* [1960] 2 Q.B. 430, 441, suggesting the contrary cannot be accepted, especially since *The Wagon Mound (No. 1)* [1961] A.C. 388. For criticism, see Jolowicz [1960] C.L.J. 156.

[94] [1983] A.C. 410.
[95] *Schneider v. Eisovitch, supra.*
[96] *Bourhill v. Young* [1943] A.C. 92, where the plaintiff was a stranger and her act in going to the spot where the collision occurred was prompted by curiosity.

Discussion of Nervous Shock: Clerk & Lindsell

CLERK & LINDSELL
PARAGRAPH

10-07　**Recognised kind of harm**
NOTE 51. Add after the reference to *Emeh* and before the reference to *McKay*: In *Thake* v. *Maurice* [1986] Q.B. 644, Pain J. whose decision was confirmed by the Court of Appeal, declined to follow *Udale* and awarded damages for the cost of bringing up the child. In *Benarr* v. *Kettering Health Authority* (1988) 138 New L.J. 179, the damage award included a sum for the future private education of the "unwanted" child. For a full survey of the case law in this area, see Symmons, "Policy factors in actions for wrongful birth" (1987) 50 M.L.R. 269–306.

10-08　**Damage to the person**
NOTE 55. Add: The common law *lacuna* has now been filled by the decision in *B. v. Islington Health Authority* [1991] 1 All E.R. 825 where dealing with a gynaecological operation on a pregnant woman prior to the passing of the 1976 Act, it was held that the plaintiff who was born with abnormalities as a result of the operation had a common law action in negligence. In reaching his decision Potts J. stated that the general test for duty in cases involving physical injury was the foresight of the reasonable man and that this test was unaffected by economic loss decisions such as *Caparo Industries plc* v. *Dickman* and *Murphy* v. *Brentwood D.C.*

10-10　**Nervous shock**
It should also be noted that the phrase "nervous shock" does not carry its lay meaning of a short, unpleasant stimulus, but a narrower legal meaning of psychiatric illness. Indeed, in *Attia* v. *British Gas*[63a] Bingham L.J. criticised the use of the phrase "nervous shock" saying the he would "use the general expression 'psychiatric damage' intending to comprehend within it all the relevant forms of mental illness, neurosis and personality change." The plaintiff must show that the psychiatric illness was caused by a "reaction to an immediate and horrifying impact" for which the defendant was responsible. The law has not so far recognised a claim where the psychiatric illness resulted from an "accumulation of more gradual assaults upon the nervous system" stemming from the defendant's conduct.[63b] Nor is it enough to show that the event caused stress which contributed to the plaintiff's suffering psychiatric illness in reaction to a subsequent shocking event.[63c] Ward J. has recently commented that the need to prove causation of psychiatric illness is the "first hurdle" which "not many will jump" and this should allay "fears of the floodgates opening too wide."[63d] Mere stress or anxiety will not give rise to a nervous shock action[63e] although compensation for anxiety may awarded where, exceptionally, the defendant's duty to the plaintiff involves giving peace of mind.[63f]
NOTE 63a. [1988] Q.B. 304 and see *Ravenscroft* v. *Rederiaktiebolaget Transatlantic* [1991] 3 All E.R. 73 at 76.
NOTE 63b. *Jones* v. *Wright* [1991] 3 All E.R. 88, C.A., at p. 123 *per* Nolan L.J; [1991] 4 All E.R. 907, *per* Lords Keith and Ackner (*sub nom. Alcock* v. *Chief Constable of the South Yorkshire Police*).
NOTE 63c. *Campbelltown C.C.* v. *McKay* (1988) 15 N.S.W.L.R. 501, N.S.W.C.A. The plaintiff had suffered stress following the collapse of her "dream house" due to the defendants' negligence, but her psychiatric illness followed a still birth which was unrelated to her stress. The plaintiff failed to recover nervous shock damages, but she did recover the equivalent sum as damages for distress and anxiety resulting from the collapse of the house.
NOTE 63d. *Ravenscroft* v. *Rederiaktiebolaget Transatlantic* [1991] 3 All E.R. 73 at 76.
NOTE 63e. Thus in *De Franceschi* v. *Storrier* (1989) 85 A.L.R./A.C.T.R. 1, it was held that a parent could not recover for mere anxiety about her children who had suffered in an accident. However, she was able to recover for the extent to which the anxiety had prolonged the effect of the original shock.
NOTE 63f. See NOTE 63b *supra* and § 11–45, NOTE 83, *post.*

Clerk & Lindsell Supplement

CLERK & LINDSELL
PARAGRAPH

10-11   Delete first paragraph and substitute: The second aspect of shock, *i.e.* whether there is a limit on the type of plaintiff who is entitled to recover, was considered by the House of Lords in *Alcock* v. *Chief Constable of the South Yorkshire Police.*[79] The plaintiffs had suffered psychiatric illness following the Hillsborough stadium disaster at which friends or relatives had been killed or injured. The relationship of the plaintiffs to the victims included a wife, parents, sisters, brothers, uncles, a grandfather, a brother-in-law, a fiancée and a friend. Giving the leading speech, Lord Keith said:

> "As regards the class of persons to whom a duty may be owed . . . I think it sufficient that reasonable foreseeability should be the guide. I would not seek to limit the class by reference to particular relationships such as husband and wife or parent and child. The kinds of relationship which may involve close ties of love and affection are numerous . . . They may be present in family relationships or those of close friendship, and may be stronger in the case of engaged couples than in that of persons who have been married to each other for many years. It is common knowledge that such ties exist, and reasonably foreseeable that those bound by them may in certain circumstances be at real risk of psychiatric illness if the loved one is injured or put in peril. The closeness of the tie would, however, require to be proved by a plaintiff, though no doubt being capable of being presumed in appropriate cases. Psychiatric damage to [a bystander] would not ordinarily be within the range of reasonable foreseeability, but could not perhaps be entirely excluded from it if the circumstances of a catastrophe occuring very close to him were particularly horrific."

This approach with which Lord Ackner agreed, would justify recovery in appropriate cases by siblings,[80] fiancés,[81] friends and exceptionally, bystanders.[82]

Applying this approach, Lord Keith rejected claims by plaintiffs who lost brothers, a brother-in-law, and a grandson, on the ground that there was insufficient evidence of close ties of love and affection. However, in the case of plaintiffs whose son was killed and a plaintiff who lost her fiancé, he held that "the closest ties of love and affection fall to be presumed from the fact of the particular relationship and there is no suggestion of anything which might tend to rebut that presumption." Their claims failed on the ground that the scenes they witnessed on television could not reasonably be regarded as giving rise to shock.[83] The line between those relationships which are so close as to give rise to a rebuttable presumption in favour of "the closest ties of love and affection" and those where such a tie will have to be positively proved, may be of crucial importance in future cases. Lord Keith's speech suggests that the former category may be narrowly confined to spouses/fiancés and parents.

NOTE 79. [1991] 4 All E.R. 907.

NOTE 80. *The Devonshire Maid* [1952] 2 Lloyd's Rep. 95.

NOTE 81. *Currie* v. *Wardrop* 1927 S.C. 538.

NOTE 82. An obvious example is *Chadwick* v. *British Railways Board* [1967] 1 W.L.R. 912 in which the plaintiff, a rescuer, was held entitled to recover for shock even though he was in no way related to the dead and injured whom he helped to rescue but where he had to perform his acts of rescue in a horrifying situation. It would seem more appropriate to explain the decision in *Dooley* v. *Cammell Laird & Co. Ltd.* [1952] 1 Lloyd's Rep. 721, where a plaintiff who recovered for shock suffered through seeing his workmates endangered could, on the basis of the particularly horrific circumstances (the plaintiff's crane suddenly dropped a load on his workmates) rather than any supposed closeness of emotional tie between workmates.

NOTE 83. See *infra*, § 10–13.

27

10–12   NOTE 89. Add: In *Ravenscroft* v. *Rederiaktiebolaget Transatlantic* [1991] 3 All E.R. 73, expert evidence established that the plaintiff had a "normal standard of susceptibility" and that her suffering following her son's death was "a little unusual but not abnormal."

NOTE 91. Add: See also *Hevican* v. *Ruane* [1991] 3 All E.R. 65.

NOTE 94. Add: Two first instance decisions have extended recovery beyond the immediate aftermath situation recognised in *McLoughlin*. In *Hevican* v. *Ruane* [1991] 3 All E.R. 65, a father who suffered reactive depression produced by the news of his son's death, the sight of his body in the mortuary and the continuing sense of loss, was held entitled to recover. Mantell J. commented that "it would be stretching language beyond all bounds to say that the plaintiff's condition is as a result of coming upon the accident's immediate aftermath." In *Ravenscroft* v. *Rederiaktiebolaget Transatlantic* [1991] 3 All E.R. 73, Ward J. went further, allowing a mother to recover when she had been told of her son's death shortly after the accident but did not see the body. He admitted that the facts were "way beyond the margin" of the immediate aftermath but argued that the caselaw suggested that "the move has been away from the geographical confines of the zone of danger and the focus should now switch to the closeness of the relationship and the considerations of casual proximity." In *Alcock* v. *Chief Constable of the South Yorkshire Police* [1991] 4 All E.R. 907 Lord Keith after citing Lord Wilberforce's view that the law should not compensate shock brought about by communication with a third party, commented that: "On that basis it is open to serious doubt whether *Hevican* and *Ravenscroft* were correctly decided, since in both of these cases the effective cause of the psychiatric illness would appear to have been the fact of a son's death and the news of it." However, the phrasing of this comment suggests that the key factor was not the "immediate aftermath" nor even the third party communication, but rather that the cause of the shock was the death and not the appreciation of the horrifying event causing the death.

Delete last nine lines of section and substitute:

The question concerning sight or hearing through simultaneous television was considered by the House of Lords in *Alcock* v. *Chief Constable of the South Yorkshire Police*.[96a] It was held that perception of the shocking event "through the broadcast of selective images accompanied by commentary" did not satisfy the proximity test. Lords Keith and Ackner emphasised that the televised scenes did not depict the suffering of recognisable individuals, such scenes being excluded by the broadcasting code of ethics.[96b] Hence, they concluded that although such scenes could give rise to "anxiety and distress," they could not "reasonably be regarded as giving rise to shock, in the sense of a sudden assault on the nervous system." Viewing such scenes could not be equated with "the sight or hearing of the event or its immediate aftermath." However, Lord Ackner went on to agree with the view of Nolan L.J. in the Court of Appeal that "simultaneous broadcasts of a disaster cannot in all cases be ruled out as providing the equivalent of the actual sight or hearing of the event or its immediate aftermath." Lord Ackner cited the example given by Nolan L.J. of a publicity-seeking organisation arranging an event involving children travelling in a balloon and for the televising of the event so that their parents could watch. In that situation there could be liability to parents suffering shock on seeing the simultaneous television pictures of the balloon crashing, for the impact on the parents would be "as great if not greater than the actual sight of the accident."

Whether a similar approach could be taken to shock produced by a third party's information is more doubtful. In *Ravenscroft* v. *Rederiaktiebolaget Transatlantic*,[96c] decided prior to *Alcock*, Ward J. held that there could be sufficient proximity where the plaintiff's perception was based entirely upon what she had been told by

28

a third party. The mother's imagination of the horrific manner of her son's death made up for the lack of direct perception. The decision in *Ravenscroft* was doubted by Lord Keith in *Alcock*. Lord Keith cited Lord Wilberforce's statement in *McLoughlin* that the "law should not compensate shock brought about by communication with a third party" but his express reason for doubting *Ravenscroft* was that "the effective cause of the psychiatric illness would appear to have been the fact of a son's death and the news of it." It is suggested that in some situations the impact of third party communication could be "as great as the actual sight of the accident" and that the real problem in such situations is whether the way in which the information is communicated, *e.g.* insensitively, is such as to break the chain of causation.[96d]

NOTE 96a. [1991] 4 All E.R. 907.

NOTE 96b. It appears from the speech of Lord Ackner that counsel for the plaintiffs conceded that had the television pictures shown suffering by recognisable individuals, this would have been "a *novus actus* breaking the chain of causation between the chief constable's alleged breach of duty and the psychiatric illness."

NOTE 96c. [1991] 3 All E.R. 73.

NOTE 96d. See the concession of counsel above, note 96b.

10–13A   A helpful analysis of nervous shock liability is provided by the judgment of Ward J. in *Ravenscroft* v. *Rederiaktiebolaget Transatlantic*.[96e] After noting that the plaintiff had to show that the defendant's conduct had caused psychiatric illness and that the steps in the chain of causation were all reasonably foreseeable *ex post facto*, Ward J. turned to the basis of the defendant's duty. He argued that what distinguished shock from other personal injury cases was the fact that the damage was indirect, the direct damage being that caused to the loved one. It was this indirect nature of the nexus which required the plaintiff to establish proximity as well as reasonable foreseeability of illness. In judging reasonable foreseeability, the court should take into account the plaintiff's physical closeness in time and space to the accident, the means by which the shock was caused, *e.g.* by sight, hearing or subsequent communication, and the relationship of the plaintiff to the victim of the accident.[96f] The weight to be given to these three factors was a matter for judgment from case to case. In judging proximity the court had to consider whether there was such a relation between the parties that it was fair, just and reasonable to impose liability. This involved a consideration of policy factors such as whether the imposition of damages would be out of proportion to the negligent conduct complained of.[96g] It also involved considering the existing categories of liability and deciding whether the law could be developed "incrementally and by analogy" from these to encompass the relationship in question. Currents of judicial opinion favouring the plaintiff and cross-currents favouring no liability had to be evaluated. Finally, the Judge had to take a decision in the light of these common law principles.

NOTE 96e. [1991] 3 All E.R. 73.

NOTE 96f. The three factors mentioned by Tobriner J. in *Dillon* v. *Legg* (1968) 68 Cal. 2d 728 at 740, and applied by Lord Bridge in *McLoughlin* v. *O'Brian*.

NOTE 96g. Parker L.J. justified the rejection of the plaintiffs' claims in *Jones* v. *Wright* [1991] 3 All E.R. 88, on this policy ground.

10–16 Economic loss

NOTE 7. Add: See too, on recent developments, Huxley, (1990) 53 M.L.R. 369 and Stapleton, (1991) 107 L.Q.R. 249. See also the comment of Lord Brandon in *The Hua Lien* [1991] 1 Lloyd's Rep. 309, 328–329: "in most claims in respect of physical damage to property the question of the existence of a duty of care does not give rise to any problem, because it is self-evident that such a duty exists and the contrary view is unarguable." Similar statements can be found in *Caparo* v. *Dick-*

Clerk & Lindsell Supplement

in particular. She should check The Current Law Case Citator and The Law Reports Index. Then she should check that case in the Case Citator and in the 'Cases Considered' part of the index.

Finally, to be absolutely sure nothing important has been decided in the last months, Laura should check the daily newspaper reports.

Laura should look at the case report itself or any relevant cases, and not just the headnotes.

Computers and Legal Research

Legal research is rapidly becoming automated. Push a button and see a case, flip a switch and read a statute—well, almost. But certain legal research tasks that might take hours or days in the law library can now be accomplished in minutes with the help of computers.

However, book lovers take heart—it does not appear that silicon chips will take the place of well-stocked law libraries, at least for many years to come. For reasons discussed later in the chapter, the computer-assisted legal research systems now available can profitably be used only by persons already skilled in legal analysis and research.

Most people use systems to supplement, and not replace, written materials. The primary reason for this is that using a computer-assisted legal research system requires a way of thinking that is fundamentally different than the one most legal researchers have learned. Access to computerised materials is gained by searching for specific key words actually used in them. The idea of asking a question by anticipating the words in the answer is utterly foreign to most of us.

The other major factors affecting the use of computer-assisted legal research systems are their restricted availability and their cost.

Especially if you are not connected with a law office or law school, you may have extreme difficulty in obtaining access to Lexis. Most public law libraries do not offer these services. Those that do require a sizeable advance deposit or a credit card; you pay as you go. If you nonetheless wish to use one of these systems, ask your law librarian where the nearest publicly accessible terminal is located.

If you do find an available service, be prepared for another shock. You can end up paying as much as £1 a minute, but pricing may vary significantly.

A   How Lexis Works

When it comes to legal research, a computer cannot do anything you could not do given enough time. It can only do some things a lot faster.

The legal research computers are great at storing huge amounts of information and retrieving specific items very quickly. That's it— that's all they do. You cannot type your legal problem into Lexis and expect an answer. But you can type in specific words that are central to your problem and have the computer find every reference to those words in its huge memory.

This memory contains, among other things, almost all reported cases, regulations, law review articles, commonly used treatises and practice manuals. All the information is stored in a central computer; the Lexis terminals found in law libraries and offices are connected to this computer by phone lines. Users of private micro-computers and word processors (for example, IBM PC, Macintosh, Wang) can also tie into the central computer if they have the proper communication equipment and software, and can pay for the privilege.

The computer's memory is organised into 'databases', or electronic files. One database may contain all cases, another all statutes, and another all regulations. You must therefore specify both where to search (what database) and what to search for (specific words) when you use Lexis. For example, if your legal problem involves sport and negligence, you might ask Lexis for every case that contains the words 'sport' and 'negligence'. The computer will search all the information in its database of cases and in seconds pull out every case that uses those words. You will get nothing more, nothing less. You will not get cases that involve negligence and drink-driving, even though they may be indirectly relevant to your problem.

B   How to Use Lexis Economically

Without a doubt, the single biggest impediment to using Lexis is the prohibitive expense. If you are not careful you could run up a bill of £50 and end up with no more than a few marginally relevant cases. This cost/benefit ratio associated with computerised legal research often has the additional negative effect of making you worry about the 'ticking of the meter'. Because legal research commonly involves a mixture of concentration on finding materials and reflection on where to go next, anything that disturbs your mental processes is highly undesirable.

The charges are based on the length of time you are connected with the system and the number of times the words that you are using to access material are used in the database (the more times the words appear, the more work the machine has to do to find what you are looking for).

Fortunately, you can take steps to minimise the cost of your research and maximise your results. While you may not want to read a case on the screen leisurely, you may save dozens of hours of work.

1 Learn how to use the system in advance

Lexis has modules that permit you to self-train at the terminal without charge. You should spend at least five hours going through these modules before even thinking about doing the real thing. The more proficient you are in switching from one database to another, using the commands associated with the particular system and knowing how to formulate your queries, the more efficient your search will be.

2 Plan your search

The typical legal research task is most efficiently carried out by making use of both written materials and those in a computer database. First, decide what information you want. In many instances, the information may be readily available in written form. It will usually make no sense for you to use a computer to read the article if the written volume can easily be obtained. It is often as quick to read the printed words as to call up the same material on the screen, and a lot cheaper.

Once you decide which type of information you wish to search for with the help of the computer, work out which database or databases to use. While Lexis allows you to switch easily from one database to another, a search conducted in the wrong database will be money down the drain. Finally, have your search query written out and in front of you.

C   Choosing a Database

After you 'sign on' to Lexis (the librarian will show you how to do this), the first thing you must do is tell the computer which of its databases you want searched. The computer will give you a 'menu' of choices that go from the general to the specific. For example, if you choose 'Statutes' from the first set of options, you will then be asked to choose from a sub-menu. Of, if you already know your way around the system a little bit and know what database you want, you can issue a direct command (check the manual for the exact way to do this).

Of course, you can go from one database to another and ultimately search every one, but a multi-database search can get quite expensive.

D   Formulating your Query

The key to getting information out of Lexis is knowing what questions to ask. And the key to getting information that you can afford is drafting these questions in advance of asking them—what we call 'formulating your query'. Here we provide a brief overview of how you do this. More detailed information is available from the database provider.

1   Choosing your key words

A well thought-out query is one designed to net just the right number of relevant cases. This requires the same type of word-finding skill as that discussed in Chapter 4, Putting your Questions into Legal Categories. Only here, instead of accessing information according to its type or kind, you must figure about what actual words are likely to be used in the particular document you need (for example, case, statute or law review article) and then call it up by these words.

For example, suppose you own a restaurant that specialises in apple pie made from a recipe developed by your great-great-great-grandmother. One day your baker resigns and takes up employment down the street, where she starts producing the same apple pie that you have always considered your proprietary secret. You want to find out whether you have a right to prevent your competitor from selling pies made from your recipe. If you were using conventional legal research techniques, you would find a legal encyclopaedia or book specialising in 'intellectual property' or 'trade secrets' and look in the index under 'employees', injunctions', 'recipes' and so on. With a little effort, you would soon find some relevant material.

If you were using Lexis to accomplish the same task, however, you could not use these concepts to find what you were looking for unless these very words were actually used in a case, statute or article. Put simply, you cannot tell the computer to find cases about trade secrets and recipes. Instead, you have to tell the computer to search for cases according to the words the case uses.

If you did tell the computer to search for cases using the terms 'trade secret' and 'recipes', you would get only cases that use both those exact terms. The computer would not give you an opinion that fails to use these terms but does mention 'business know-how' and 'culinary information'. On the other hand, if your request requires the computer to search for cases containing any of these terms (and more if you can think of them), the chances that you will find any case on point in the database you are searching are excellent. Of course, if you give the computer too many words that individually will produce a reference, then you will get more material than you can reasonably use. Again, the trick to using Lexis is to pull up just the right amount of relevant material.

2 Using connectors

Lexis uses a system of 'connectors' that let you design an efficient query. With connectors you can specify that you only want to see cases that have certain key words in the same sentence or paragraph, or you can exclude documents that contain certain other words. How to use specific connectors is explained below.

Lexis Connectors

The following connectors are used by Lexis:

W/n   The means 'within a particular number of words.'
             Thus, 'strict w/1 liability' means 'strict' within
             one word of 'liability'. Given this command, the
             computer with retrieve documents with either
             'strict liability' or 'liability strict'. If the command
             were W/10, the computer would retrieve all
             documents in which the two words appeared
             within 10 words of each other.

And   This means that the item being searched must
             contain the words on either side of And.
             Accordingly, 'noise And nuisance' means the item
             being searched must contain both the word 'noise'
             and the word 'nuisance'. Otherwise Lexis will not
             produce it.

Or   This means that the item being searched must
             contain either the word that comes before or the
             word that comes after. Accordingly, 'noise Or
             nuisance' will produce items that contain either
             the term noise or the term nuisance.

Pre/n   This means that the item being searched must
             contain both the word before the connector and
             the word after the connector and that the word
             before the connector must come first. Accordingly,
             'quiet pre/1 enjoyment means that the item being
             searched must contain the term 'quiet enjoyment'.

And Not   This means that the term following this connector
             cannot be in the case. This is used when you do
             not want to be bothered with a certain type of case.
             Thus, 'child pre/1 custody And Not joint' means
             that you want to see cases on child custody but
             none that involve joint custody.

Reminder Do not worry about learning these commands and
connectors. Our purpose here is to give you an overview of how this

all works. When you sit down at a Lexis terminal, you should have the user's manual by your side. A knowledgeable law librarian and an on-line training module provided by Lexis should also help you get started.

Here are several examples of typical queries with Lexis connectors, just to give you a feel:

Example 1 You want a listing of every case that has used the terms 'employment' and 'discrimination'. If the order in which these terms were used was not important to you, your query would look like this: employment *and* discrimination. If you only wanted cases that used the phrase 'employment discrimination', your request would read: employment pre/1 discrimination.

Example 2 You want to see every case that has discussed safety standards in low-income housing. Your query might read as follows: moderate or low w/5 income *and* safety w/20 housing. This would tend to produce all cases that linked the words 'moderate' or 'low' with 'income' and the word 'safety' with 'housing'.

Example 3 You want to see all cases dealing with decertification of non-agricultural unions. You could use the following query: decertification w/10 union *and not* agriculture.

3 Using universal characters and root extenders

Part of the art of writing a good query is knowing when and how to use the universal character (the asterisk) and the root extender (the exclamation mark).

Let us take the asterisk first. This character serves a function similar to that of a wild card in poker. When you insert it in a word in a query, it stands for any character occupying that position in the word. Suppose, for example, your search involves women's rights. You would want to include the term women in your search query, but would also want to capture cases that use the term woman. If you only listed 'women', you might miss some important cases. By using the asterisk, you can have the computer search for all cases (for example) containing the term 'wom*n'. This would produce cases with both women and woman.

The exclamation point provides even more flexibility. It must be placed at the end of the word, which instructs the computer to select all documents that contain the string of characters (root) just prior to it. For example, the term 'Manag!' would pick up manage, management, manager and managers.

4 Modifying your query

It is unusual for even experienced researchers to get their queries right the first time around. Instead their initial selection of words either produces too many cases or too few. For example, if you asked to see all national cases with the terms 'environmental' and 'impact' (used in an example above), your search would produce many hundreds of cases, too many for you reasonably to review. You would need to modify your search so that it would provide fewer, but all relevant, cases. If your situation involves a nuclear power plant, you would modify your search to include only cases that use environmental and impact and nuclear and power plant.

On the other hand, if your initial query is too restrictive, you may have to drop a term or two to produce any relevant documents. As a general rule, the more words that must be in a case as requested (for example, every case with the words 'drunk' and 'intoxicated' and 'under the influence'), the fewer cases will be found, since any case that does not have all the required terms would not be produced. Conversely, the fewer and more general the words in a query that must be in a case to retrieve it (for example, every case with the word 'eviction') the more cases will be produced.

5 Doing segment searches

As you learned earlier, a reported case really consists of a number of different elements. The main one, of course, is the written opinion itself. However there are also the case name, the headnotes, the date the case was decided, the name of the judge who wrote the opinion, the title of the court deciding the case and so on.

Lexis allows you to search documents by reference to these segments. Thus, if you want to retrieve all cases of a specific type decided by a particular judge, you can do so. Or, if you know you are looking for a Court of Appeal case decided between 1972 and 1975, you can specify these dates in your query and the computer will perform the search.

6 Choosing which portions of a document to review

When you turn up cases during your research, you must sift through them to see if they are useful. When you are looking in books, this sifting generally involves reading the headnotes, finding one or more that looks relevant and reading the portion of the opinion from which the headnote was taken.

When you use Lexis to do legal research, you can do this same type of sifting. Once the computer has responded to your query and located documents containing your search words, you can designate which part of the document you wish to look at. You may choose to see just the portion where you key words appear. Or you may choose to see the entire page.

Money Saving Tips

Once you are using the system, there are some techniques that will help you get in and out as quickly as possible.

Use Field Browsing Seldom should you read an entire case on the screen. Make liberal use of the option to just view the portion of the document where the key terms appear. If the document looks relevant, note its citation and look up the printed report later. By using this browsing or skimming technique, you can cover a lot of ground in only a few minutes. This will save you money.

Use your Printer You can print out any material you discover in your search that looks promising. You are not charged while the printing is being done. Thus if you find a case that looks relevant, but do not have easy access to it in a library, you can print it for later reference. However, cases are generally much easier to read in the published reports. Accordingly, print only when time is a factor or your access to the published document is limited.

7   Updating a selected document and finding similar documents

Among the greatest advantages of Lexis is that its databases are very up–to–date. While it may take several months for a relevant case to show up in digests, these computerised services are likely to receive it within a week or two after it is decided, or even sooner. It is comforting to know that your information is completely rather than almost up–to–date.

We saw in earlier chapters that the citators and the case digests can be used both to update cases and to find other cases involving similar facts and issues. Because you can search the Lexis databases for any specific character or number, it is extremely easy to find out whether a particular case or statute you are concerned with has been referred to by another case. For example, if the citation to your case is [1982] AC 1105, you can check all subsequent cases for that reference and then scan the portion where it occurs to see whether the citing case is relevant. Put simply, by just sitting at your terminal, you can not only find relevant cases (or other material) but can also check for its continued validity and search out other materials that are similar. (See Chapter 8 and 9 on how to do this manually.)

Computerised Legal Research at a Glance

•   Computer–assisted legal research focuses by telling the computer to select only those materials that fit the criteria specified in the search request.

•   A computer search request must anticipate which words are used in the document being searched, and their position relative to one another (for example, same sentence, or within 20 words of each other). Connectors and universal characters are used to do this.

•   Generally, the fewer and more general the key words the query requires to be in the document being searched, the more material will be produced. The more key words required to be in the document, and the more specific they are, the fewer the materials that will be found.

- The ultimate objective in query formulation is to narrow the search enough, but not too much.

E   The Future of Computers and Self-Help Law

It is clearly only a matter of time until anyone with access to a computer will also have access to many different types of specialised legal databases. Some of these will be accessed over the phone line in the same way as the Lexis system.

This is not a pie-in-the-sky dream. Already there are self-help law computer programmes allowing you to make your own will or living trust, form your own corporation, draft your own contracts and produce your own tailor-made partnership agreement. Many more are on the drawing boards. However, such single-application programmes are not enough for a true street corner law machine. We need the ability to store large amounts of material and a programme that is able to interact with the user in a human-like manner (artificial intelligence). Fortunately, such developments as laser disk technology allow the physical storage of the database, and several new database management programmes allow the easy retrieval of information through the use of English language commands. In addition, great strides have been made in development tools that allow the construction of expert systems—computer programmes that emulate experts such as doctors, lawyers and mining engineers.

Concisely put, there are now no technological or intellectual impediments to the development and operation of a street corner law machine along the lines suggested here.

Given its feasibility, then, and the cost of lawyers' services, why doesn't a street corner law machine already exist on every corner? The answer, unfortunately, is not simple. Part of the problem is the sheer amount of time necessary to organise and link information in a way that will facilitate its retrieval by the law machine user. Despite the fact that many excellent self-help law books are on the market, the format of a good book does not necessarily convert to an efficient database.

REVIEW

Questions

1   Why is the use of computerised legal research systems limited?

2   If you select the database for national cases and ask Lexis to search for the word 'bicycle', what will you get?

3   What are two ways to use Lexis economically?

4   In using Lexis, if you use the connector AND with the words 'bicycle' and 'accident', what will Lexis produce?

5   If you list 'bicycl!' what would Lexis pick up?

6   How can you use the system to update your research?

Answers

1   The primary reason for this is that using a computer-assisted legal research system requires a way of thinking that is fundamentally different from the one most legal researchers have learned. Access to computerised materials is gained by searching for specific key words actually used in them. The idea of asking a question by anticipating the words in the answer is utterly foreign to most of us. The other major factors affecting the use of computer-assisted legal research systems are their restricted availability and their cost.

2   All national cases in which the opinion includes the word 'bicycle' somewhere.

3   First, learn how to use the system in advance. Then, plan your search before you 'sign on'.

4   Items in which both words appear, in any order.

5   Bicycle, bicyclist, bicycling.

6   By checking all subsequent cases for references to your case.

Appendix 1

Appendix 1 contains a research hypothetical. It presents a set of facts and a research question that provides the basis for a research exercise which will take you to legislation and case law. The exercise consists of a research problem involving a number of questions which require answering. The answers will be given in the form of a legal memorandum, without the repetition of facts and questions involved.

At the beginning of the exercise is a list of the resources necessary to answer the questions – they should be available in most law libraries. Appendix 2 contains two further research exercises intended to sharpen your research skills.

a) The facts

Mr Stevens is the defendant (D) in a criminal matter. He has been charged with an offence under the Trade Descriptions Act, that is he produced and sold yoghurt which was described as 'natural', yet allegedly contained artificial ingredients. The prosecutor is the Alderly County Council. D has been summoned to appear at the Hillow Magistrates Court in two weeks.

D was summoned to court by a summons dated 25 April, 1993. However, the summons did not arrive until 29 April. A letter was sent on 15 April asking D to be interviewed on 27 April. He was interviewed by the County Council on 27 April, but he was unaware at that time that he had been summoned.

The letter of 15 April stated that the interview would be conducted in accordance with the provisions of The Police And Criminal Evidence Act 1984. However, D was not cautioned and was not told of the summons.

During the course of the interview, in an attempt to dissuade the County Council from continuing with their prosecution, D revealed some of his expert's evidence relating to the contents of the yoghurt products. This information was used by the Council's expert to produce a second report before trial.

On 29 April, D received the summons and became worried about the information he had given away.

b) The questions

You are D's defence counsel or solicitor. Is there any way to keep the magistrates from hearing about or reading the interview? Would excluding the interview be of any use to D? Is there any way that the prosecution could be stopped completely?

c) The resources to consider

Current Law Statutes Annotated

Halsbury's Statutes

'The Police And Criminal Evidence Act' - Michael Zander

Archbold - 'Criminal Procedure, Evidence And Practice'

The Current Law Case Citator

The Law Reports Index

Keane - 'The Modern Law of Evidence'

d) The answers

LEGAL MEMORANDUM

To: Peter Vox (solicitor for D)

From: Sarah Carter (trainee solicitor)

Topic: Mr Stevens' defence.

Conclusion

It would be possible to argue that D's interview with the County Council should be excluded by the magistrates under section 78 of The Police And Criminal Evidence Act 1984 (PACE). The Council told D they would abide by the provisions of PACE yet did not caution him. They also interviewed him after he had been summoned, which is tantamount to the police interviewing him after they have cautioned him. However, I do not believe the admission of the interview would prejudice D in any way, as he made no damaging admissions. More importantly, it may be possible to persuade the magistrates that the prosecution should be stopped in its tracks and the summons dismissed due to abuse of process.

Reasoning

Section 78 of PACE states that the court may exclude any evidence the prosecution proposes to rely on if it appears to the court, having regard to all the circumstances, including the circumstances in which the evidence was obtained, that the admission would have such an adverse effect on the fairness of the proceedings that the court ought not to admit it. This power is in addition to the common law power of exclusion provided by *R v Sang* [1980] AC 402.

In the present case there has been a breach of paragraph 10.1 of Code C of PACE. This states that a suspect must be cautioned before being interviewed by the police – ie before any questions are put to him which are for the purpose of obtaining evidence which may become part of the Prosecution's case. Clearly, a caution was needed in the present case.

There has also been a breach of paragraph 16.5 of Code C of PACE. This states that after a person has been charged by the police, they can no longer be questioned unless such questioning is necessary to prevent or minimise harm or loss to some other person or to the public, or for clearing up an ambiguity in a previous answer or statement, or where it is in the interests of justice that the person should be allowed to answer or comment on information concerning the offence which has come to light since the D was charged. Clearly, none of these exceptions apply to Mr Stevens' case, especially as this was his first interview.

With these two breaches, section 78 of PACE should allow for the exclusion of the interview. Examples of cases where exclusion of interview evidence has occurred due to breaches of the Codes of PACE include *R v Keenan* [1989] 3 All ER 598 (recording of interviews); *R v Foster* [1987] Crim LR 821 (no contemporaneous note, in breach of the Codes of PACE); and *R v Saunders* [1988] Crim LR 521 (caution worded wrongly). *R v Keenan* (above) makes it clear that bad faith on the part of the police may make a substantial difference to the question of exclusion, but good faith does not cure breaches which are significant. In the present case it may well be accepted that the breach of paragraph 16.5 is significant.

However, although it may make the Prosecution's case more difficult if the point on section 78 is argued, the interview does not contain anything that D will not want the magistrates to hear during the trial. It would make more sense to attempt to persuade the magistrates to dismiss the summons as to allow the case to go ahead would be abuse of process.

The starting point for abuse of process is *R v Derby Crown Court, ex p Brooks* (1985) 80 Cr App R 164. Although this case concerns delay in bringing the prosecution, it lays down the principle circumstances in which abuse of process applies, including where the Prosecution have manipulated the process of the court so as to deprive the defendant of a protection provided by the law or to take an unfair advantage of a technicality. (See pages 168/169.)

Brooks was applied in *R v Bow Street Stipendiary Magistrate, ex p Director of Public Prosecutions* (1990) 91 Cr App R 283. Again, this involved delay on the part of the Prosecution, but in it Watkins LJ approves the principle laid down in *Brooks* (at page 295). Further, in the case of *Attorney-General's Reference (No 1 of 1990)* [1992] 1 QB 630, the Court of Appeal applies *Brooks* to another case of delay. This case places the burden of proving prejudice as the result of the abuse of process on the defendant. The standard is on the balance of probabilities. The Court of Appeal also hold that in the absence of fault on the part of the Prosecution, it will be all the more difficult to stop a prosecution continuing.

All of the above cases emphasise that an abuse of process argument will only allow the prosecution to be dropped in exceptional circumstances. This may be such a case in that the Prosecution's expert was given the opportunity before the trial to produce a second report as a result of the interview of D. One would assume that he would not have agreed to the interview had he known of the summons.

As the Defence present their case after the conclusion of the Prosecution's case, the Prosecution have obtained an unfair advantage over D here as they can respond to D's expert evidence before it is given. This, of course, is a fundamental breach of the right to silence. This prejudice to D cannot be cured in any way, as the prosecution expert will be giving evidence as well as producing her report.

Even if the interview was held in the mistaken belief that D knew about the summons, I believe D has a strong argument for exclusion.

Of course, if the prosecution is stopped there is nothing to stop the County Council from buying another yoghurt and starting the process again.

Appendix 2

Appendix 2 contains two more research exercises. The first is concerned with legislation and procedure; the second with case law. At this stage you should not be worried about the time it takes you to find the correct answers—what is important is that you do find relevant legislation and case law. Again, the answer will be given in the form of a legal memorandum, without the usual repetition of facts and questions.

EXERCISE ONE

a) The facts

An order for the payment of maintenance has been made in the English courts against Mr Elliott (E), in favour if his now ex-wife, Ms Fellows (F). E has now left the country and is residing in Mauritius. E has not paid any maintenance since he left England and F wishes to have the court order enforced.

An order for the payment of maintenance has been made against Ms Collins (C), by the English courts, in favour of Mr Huthchins (H), her now ex-husband. C has since left the country and is presently to be found in Denmark. H wishes to have the order enforced.

b) The questions

Can the maintenance orders in favour of F and H be enforced in those foreign countries? If so, how?

c) The resources

Rayden and Jackson – 'Divorce and Family Matters'

Current Law Statutes Annotated

Halsbury's Statutes

Dicey and Morris – 'Conflicts of Law'

Butterworths' Family Law Service

Halsbury's Statutory Instruments

The Legal Journals Index

d) The answers

LEGAL MEMORANDUM

To: Barry Fisher

From: Andrew Naylor

Topic: Enforcement of the maintenance orders in favour of Ms
        Fellows and Mr Huthchins.

Conclusion

Enforcement of the maintenance order in favour of Ms Fellows (F) is
possible in Mauritius, under the Maintenance Orders (Facilities for
Enforcement) Act 1920, and the Administration of Justice Act 1920.

Enforcement of the maintenance order in favour of Mr Huthchins
(H) is possible in Denmark, under Part II of the Maintenance
Orders (Reciprocal Enforcement) Act 1972, and the Civil
Jurisdiction and Judgments Act 1982.

Reasoning

The case of F

It was necessary to check whether or not there was a reciprocal enforcement arrangement between England and Mauritius. A distinction is made between lump sum payments and periodical payments. Having checked Halsbury's Statutes' index there appear to be a number of different provisions relating to enforcement of ancillary relief orders. It was really a case of looking at Rayden and checking through the different statutes in the annotated volumes, and looking at the Orders in Halsbury's Statutory Instruments and the loose-leaf S.I.s available in the library.

I eventually determined that only the Maintenance Orders (Facilities for Enforcement) Act 1920 and The Administration of Justice Act 1920 applied. I did this only to later discover an article in Family Law for November, 1992, which provided me with an instant answer. I should have checked The Legal Journals Index earlier!

The Maintenance Orders Act applies to periodical payments only. For the procedure involved in enforcement you need to look at the Family Proceedings Rules for 1991 (see Rayden). In particular, r. 7.17 is relevant. F would have to apply to a district judge to ask for registration of the order. If the district judge is satisfied that Mr Elliott (E) is residing in Mauritius, then he or she will send a copy of the registered maintenance order to the Secretary of State. The Secretary of State will then transmit a copy to the Governor of Mauritius.

The Administration of Justice Act 1920 will allow F to enforce any costs order made against E when the maintenance order was made by the English court. This Act does not apply to periodical payments.

A certified copy of the order must be obtained in the Family Division, from a district judge. This application can be made *ex parte*, and must be supported by an affidavit. See RSC. Ord. 71, r. 30. The district judge should then give F's solicitor the certified copy and the solicitor should then arrange for it to be transmitted to Mauritius for registration. The order can then be enforced.

The case of H

Part II of the Maintenance Orders (Reciprocal Enforcement) Act 1972 applies to Convention countries, of which Denmark is one. H must apply to the justice's clerk of the Secretary of State's department in order to enforce the English order in Denmark. The justice's clerk will provide assistance to H in filling in the requisite forms - the forms complying with the procedure laid down in Denmark. Once this has been done, the form is sent to the Secretary of State who will forward it to Denmark if he is satisfied that the application complies with the law of Denmark.

As Denmark is a Convention country, the Civil Jurisdiction and Judgments Act 1982 applies. 'Maintenance' obligations are covered by the Act according to Article 5(2) of the Brussels Convention which the Act brings into force. The relevant procedure is to be found in RSC Ord 71, r 36 (see the White Book). Again, there is the need to obtain a certified copy of the order from the High Court.

EXERCISE TWO

a) The facts

A is a company which acts as an employment consultant to large city firms and companies. It acts on a fixed fee basis and offers to find employees for top management posts. In this particular case, A entered into a contract with B, a solicitors firm looking for a manager for its administration department. B agreed to pay A £10,000 pounds if they found a suitable candidate who B agreed to employ. The contract stated that A would be the sole company working to fill this particular post.

A began looking for suitable candidates to interview, and had been doing this for one month when B informed A that it no longer required their services. It seems that a second company, C, had coerced B into accepting it as their exclusive employment consultant company for this particular post. C had done this by offering to find a suitable candidate for £5,000.

A does not want to sue B for breach of contract even though there has clearly been one.

A has a second complaint against C. A has been in the business of employment consultancy for years, and has throughout that time been given a regular amount of work from D, a large firm of accountants. Generally, D would enter into five or six contracts a year with A on a fixed fee basis. Recently, D has made it clear that it no longer wishes to use A. This, D says, is as the result of pressure from C, who had threatened to withdraw their services.

b) The questions

Can A sue C? How would damages be determined?

c) The resources

Clerk and Linsell on Torts (16th edition), with supplements

Salmond and Heuston on Torts

Current Law Case Citator

The Law Reports Index

The Daily Law Reports Index

d) The answers

LEGAL MEMORANDUM

To: Kerry Osborne

From: Arthur Bueno

Topic: Can A sue C in relation to the breach of contract committed by B where the only contract was between A and B.

Conclusion

A will be able to sue C for the tort of inducing breach of contract by B in relation to the contract between A and B. The damages will be measured by A's loss of profits on that contract.

As for the possible action against C in relation to D's withdrawal, an action may be possible in the tort of conspiracy or breach of Article 86 of the Treaty of Rome. As for damages, this would have to be determined by the projected loss of profits due to D's withdrawal.

The reasoning

As there is no contract between A and C there can obviously be no action for breach of contract. The only alternative is to look to the law of torts as the act committed by C is not a criminal one.

The most likely tort committed here by C is the tort of inducing breach of contract which occurs when a third party interferes with the contractual relationship between the first and second parties, to the extent that the first and second parties' contract is breached.

An action for inducing the breach of a contract is possible if A shows that an existing contract was breached; that that breach was caused by the actions of C; that C knew of the existence of the contract, and C intended to cause B to break the contract. These basic principles can be found in Clerk and Lindsell, Chapter 15.

In the present case, all these elements appear to be present. But C may attempt to argue that its intention was merely to make money out of a deal, not to break the contract between A and B - the breach was only a indirect consequence of the primary aim. But the test is an objective one once it is shown that C knew of the contract, and would seem to cover C's case. If C has dealings with the contract-breaker (here B), with knowledge of the contract between A and B, and acts in a way which it knows is inconsistent with that contract, C has committed a tort - *Thomson v Deakin* [1952] Ch 646; applied in the case of *Greig v Insole* [1978] 1 WLR 302.

As for damages, the measure of these will be the loss of profits incurred by A as a result of the breach of the contract between A and B. In this case the loss would be £10,000 less actual and anticipated expenses.

As for A's complaint against C in relation to D's withdrawal of interest, this cannot be the tort of inducing breach of contract, as D has merely refused to enter into future contracts, not broken a continuing one. There is, however, a possible action against C in conspiracy.

The tort of conspiracy will lie if A can prove that C's predominant purpose in pressurising D was to injure A, even if the actions of C were, in themselves, lawful - *Crofter Hand Woven Harris Tweed v Veitch* [1942] AC 435. The question then is, what was C's predominant purpose? C will argue that it wanted to improve its own business, not damage the business of another. This 'indirect' argument could well provide C with a defence to the tort of conspiracy by lawful means. The tort of conspiracy by unlawful means will not apply.

An alternative action may lie in the breach of Article 86 of the Treaty of Rome - ie an abuse of a dominant position in a substantial part of the common market by C. Such abuse may manifest itself by C only entering into contracts with D if D agrees to stop all business with A.

Breach of Article 86 does allow for an action in the English courts - *Garden Cottage Foods v Milk Marketing Board* [1984] A.C. 130. However, for an action on this basis to be successful, A must show that C's interference has effected trade between Member States of the Common Market. For this to occur, C must have a substantial percentage of the employment consultancy market. I therefore require more information before I can come to a conclusion on Article 86.

As for damages in this action against C in relation to D's withdrawal, these would have to be determined by A's loss of profits, as estimated, over the years A would have expected its contracts with D to continue. This, of course will be very difficult to determine, but the fact that there is a history of contractual relations is helpful.

Index